ISBN 978-0-260-28611-6
PIBN 11176461

This book is a reproduction of an important historical work. Forgotten Books uses
state-of-the-art technology to digitally reconstruct the work, preserving the original format
whilst repairing imperfections present in the aged copy. In rare cases, an imperfection in
the original, such as a blemish or missing page, may be replicated in our edition. We do,
however, repair the vast majority of imperfections successfully; any imperfections that
remain are intentionally left to preserve the state of such historical works.

1 MONTH OF
FREE
READING

at
www.ForgottenBooks.com

By purchasing this book you are eligible for one month membership to ForgottenBooks.com, giving you unlimited access to our entire collection of over 700,000 titles via our web site and mobile apps.

To claim your free month visit:
www.forgottenbooks.com/free1176461

A

TREATISE

ON

REGENERATION.

By PETER VAN MASTRICHT, *D.D.*
Profeffor of Divinity in the Univerfities of FRANCFORT,
DUISBURGH, and UTRECHT.

Extracted from his Syftem of Divinity, called Theologia theoretico-practica; and faithfully tranf-
lated into Englifh; With an APPENDIX,
containing Extracts from many celebrated Divines of the reformed Church, upon the fame
Subject.

NEW-HAVEN:

Printed and Sold by THOMAS and SAMUEL
GREEN, in the Old-Council-Chamber.

PREFACE.

THE reader will perhaps be defirous to know, who this Doct. *Van Maftricht* is, and what the particular reafons are, for publifhing the following Treatife at this time. The Publifher will endeavour, in brief to fatisfy the reader in both.

Peter Van Maftricht, author of the following Treatife ; was born in the year 1630, in the city of *Cologn*, in *Germany*, of honorable parentage, many of whofe anceftors had been confiderable fufferers in the proteftant caufe. He was educated in the univerfity of *Utrecht* ; was feveral years a preacher, in various parts of *Germany* and *Denmark* ; was invited to fettle in *Copenhagen*, capital of the latter : But was prevailed upon by the *Elector* of *Brandenburg*, (grand-father, or great-grand-father to the prefent king of *Pruffia*) to accept the place of profeffor of Hebrew and practical divinity, in his new eftablifhed univerfity at *Francfort*. He afterwards ferved in the fame ftation at *Duifburg*, near his native place ; and the laft thirty years of his life, he fuftained the fame office in the famous univerfity of *Utrecht*, the place of his education. He was greatly efteem'd as a moft accurate, judicious, learned and pious divine. He died in this office near eighty years of age. His fyftem of divinity, from whence the following Treatife is extracted, is the product of a long life, fpent in the ftudy, practice and inftruction of divinity.

The reafon for tranflating and publifhing the following Treatife at this time, is principally a hope, that it may have a tendency to put a ftop to the controverfy, which feems to be growing among us, relative to regeneration,

neration ; Whether it be wrought by the immediate influences of the divine Spirit, or by light as the means ?
and happily to unite us in the truth. The tranflator is
encouraged thus to hope, from the following confiderations,

1. He hath frequently heard gentlemen, who maintain oppofite fides of this queftion, manifeft their entire
approbation of, and concurrence with *Van Maftricht* ;
which induces him to think, that with many, the controverfy is more about terms than any thing elfe ; and
that when they find, they both can agree with *VanMaft-
richt*, they will be lead fo to explain themfelves, as to
agree with each other.

2. As our Author cannot be looked upon as partial
in favour of any particular fyftem of doctrines prevail-
ing amongft *us* ; 'tis hoped and expected that all will
read him without prejudice or partiality.

3. The great character which our author fuftains, for
which we have the ample teftimony of Dr. *Cotton Mather*,
(whofe name hath always been much refpected in the
churches of *New-England*) in the following words, ‡
" There is nothing that I can with fo much pleropho-
" rie recommend unto you, as a *Maftricht*, his *Theologia*
" *theorctico-practica.* That a minifter of the gofpel may
" be thoroughly furnifhed unto every good work, and
" in one or two quarto volumns enjoy a well furnifhed.
" library ; I know not that the fun has ever fhone up-
" on an human-compofure that is equal to it ; and I
" can heartily fubfcribe unto the commendation which
" *Pontanus*, in his *Laudatio Funebris* upon the author has
" given of it. *De hoc opere confidenter affirmo, quod eo or-
" dine fit digeftum, tanto rerum pondere pregnans et tumidum,
" tanta et tam varia eruditione refertum ; ut nefcio an in illa
" genere ufquamGentium exftet aliquid magis accuratum et ela-
" boratum.*

‡ Dr. Mather's directions for a Candidate of the miniftry. P. 85.

" boratum. † I hope you will, next unto the sacred
" scriptures, make a *Maftricht* the ftorehoufe to which
" you may refort continually. But above all things re-
" member the dying words of this true Divine; which
" he uttered *altiffima voce* (with a loud voice, and I wifh
" all that ftudy divinity might hear it!) *Se nullo loco et*
" *numero habere veritatis defenfionem, quam fincera pietas*
" *et vitæ fanctitas, individuo nexu non comitetur."* * The
character, I fay, of our Author, and his profeffedly de-
livering upon this point the general fentiment of the
whole reformed church abroad, it is hoped, will weigh
fo much, in the mind of every one, as to obtain a candid
examination of his fentiments, before they reject them.

4. Our Author's arguments are exceeding plain,
fcriptural, and convictive. There is nothing liable to
the imputation of metaphyfical nicety and fubtilty. So
far from it that his Contemporaries, who oppofed his
doctrines, " accufed him of not allowing reafon its proper place; but of dethroning it thro' pretence of religion." 'Tis therefore to be hoped, that many who have
oppofed the fentiments which our Author maintains,
from a notion of their being metaphyfical fubtilties, will
by his plain, fcriptural arguments, be convinced of the
truth of them.

5. Many, 'tis to be feared, are prejudiced againft the
doctrine which our Author endeavours to eftablifh in
the following Treatife, from a notion that it is *new* and
unheard of in the Chriftian Church. The following
Treatife,

---

† In Englifh thus. Of this work (i. e his fyftem of divinity) I
confidently affirm, that it is difpofed in that order, abounds in fuch
weighty matter, and is filled with fuch a copious variety of learning,
that I know not whether the world can afford any thing of the kind
better ftudied, and more accurate than this.

* That he hath no opinion of any defence of the truth, which
fincere piety and holinefs of life doth not infeperably accompany.

Treatife, it is hoped, will entirely remove this groundlefs objection.

But if this little Treatife fhould not prove fo fuccefsful, as to reconcile our differences upon this point, it will at leaft ferve this purpofe, to enable thofe, who have not opportunity, to look into antient authors on this fubject, to judge in fome meafure what the fentiments of the Reformed Church have been upon this important point.

Thefe confiderations induce the Tranflator ftrongly to hope, that this publication may be of happy feryice, at the prefent day. Should it in any meafure contribute to the promoting and maintaining of truth, the Tranflator will think himfelf amply rewarded for his trouble.

The Tranflator begs the candour of the Reader, with regard to the many inelegancies of ftile, which, he is apprehenfive, the critical reader will difcover in the following pages. Our Author's manner of writing is laconic, with very little decoration or ornament. A tranflation, in any meafure literal, muft refemble the genius of the original : And many Idioms of the original language will be apt infenfibly to flide into the tranflation. The Tranflator had rather forego any ornaments of ftile, which the work might receive from a more free tranflation, than thereby endanger himfelf to mifreprefent the fenfe of our Author. He hopes the Tranflation juftly reprefents the Author's fentiments, which he looks upon the principal thing ; and therefore perfuades himfelf, that any little inaccuracies of expreffion, will be kindly overlooked by the benevolent reader.

ON

ON REGENERATION.

JOHN iii. 5.

Verily, verily I say unto thee, except a man be born of Water, and of the Spirit, he cannot enter into the Kingdom of God.

I. HAVING in a former treatife difcourfed upon the *firft* act of application, in which the holy Spirit *offers* to thofe who are to be faved, for their reception, the Redeemer and Redemption. I come now to difcourfe upon the *fecond*, in which he *beftows* upon them that *power*, by which they are *enabled* to receive the offered benefits ; which is done by *regeneration*, the neceffity of which our Saviour holds forth in the words above mentioned.

THE EXPLANATORY PART.

II. Thefe words contain a weighty, powerful affertion of our Saviour, concerning the *neceffity of regeneration*. In which we may note,

1. *The perfon afferting.* I fay unto you ; *I* whom juft now you faluted by the title of *Rabbi*, or *Mafter*, a mafter *fent from God*, of which you have been convinced

B

a Ver· 2.
b Iſa. 65. 16.
c John 14. 6.
d Titus 1. 2.
Heb. 6. 18.
e John 8. 14.

f John 3. 7.

vinced by ſo many miracles ; [a] *I*, who am the *Amen*, or the God of truth ; [b] yea, the *truth* itſelf, [c] which cannot either deceive or be-deceived ; [d] whom therefore you may ſafely believe, *do aſſert, teſtify* and *declare* [e] unto you, and not only to you, but to the whole nation ; yea, and to all generations which ſhall exiſt in future ages. [f]

2. *The manner of aſſertion, amen, amen, verily, verily.* The word *amen* is of Hebrew derivation, from the root, *aman* (to be ſtable or firm) which is retained in the Greek, Syriac, Arabic, and all the Latin verſions ; and alſo in the vulgar languages. It is an adverb of *aſſerting*; that is *verily, certainly*, or the thing is ſo, or this is the *truth.* Aquila renders it, by *faithfully*; the Seventy by, *ſo be it*, but ſometimes retain the word *amen.* It is uſed either to *confirm* what hath

g Num. 5. 22.
Deut. 27. 26.
Cor. 4. 16.

been already ſpoken, [g] or to *affirm* what is now to be ſaid. The firſt uſe is moſt frequent in the old teſtament, the latter in the new. It is a particle uſed for confirmation, and is rendered either by *verily* or *ſo be it* : in the firſt ſenſe it is uſed in confirmation of ſomething *affirmed*, in the latter, in confirmation of ſomething *wiſhed* or *deſired*. If the ſentence be an *informative aſſertion*, the word means *verily or truly* ; but if *optative* or intreative, the meaning is, *ſo be it.* The particle *nai* comprehends both ſignifications ; as it is ſometimes *aſſertory*, ſometimes expreſſive of vehement deſire. Hence Luke uſeth the word *nai* (yea) for a-

h 2 Cor. 1. 17.

men. The apoſtle Paul connects them together, [h] *yea and amen* ; that one might emphatically explain the other. Our Saviour repeats the word *amen* (verily) perhaps in different ſenſes, ſo that the *firſt* may ſignify

i Iſ. 65. 16.

himſelf, I the *amen*, the *God of truth* ; [i] as it is ſaid

k Rev. 3: 14.

theſe things ſaith the *Amen, the faithful & true Witneſs.* [k] The *latter* may ſignify the truth of the thing aſſerted. So that the meaning of the expreſſion may be this, I the God of *truth* declare the *truth* unto you. It may also be designed to confirm and strengthen the truth of his paradox concerning the absolute necessity of regeneration, and the more powerfully to beget in Nicodemus a belief of the doctrine; I, the Master sent from God, verily say unto you, and that repeatedly. There are some who think the repetition of the word denotes, not a simple affirmation; but an *oath,* and that it is the same in sense with the expression, *as I live saith the Lord,* in the old testament, as the Chaldee version, for this expression, hath, as I am *constant,* stable, firm, or as I am the *amen,* the God of truth. But it doth not appear to me consistent, that one who so severely censures a rash oath, [1] should so frequently swear himself; for it is said that this expression is used fifty times by our Saviour. However, we may at least consider it as a *forcible* manner of expression, or as the Hebrews say, as *a corroboration of his words,* admirably suited to this paradox of the absolute necessity of regeneration.

   3. The thing *asserted,* with regard to which we may note,

   (1) The subject, *regeneration,* or the new-birth, "except a man be born," the same thing in ver. 2, is expressed by being born *again,* or *from above.* The word *anothen* rendered *again,* signifies sometimes, *again,* or the *second* time; thus Nicodemus seems to have understood it: [m] in which sense it occurs, Gal. 4. 9. And thus *Syrus* and *Nonnus* render it in this place. The apostle Peter useth the word *anagenethenai,* to be born again. [n] In other places the word signifies *from above,* or *from heaven.* [o] Which it seems our Saviour designed to intimate, by explaining the word *anothen* used in verse 3, by the expression *of water and of the spirit,* in verse 5, or to be born spiritually and from above, that is from heaven. What if we should connect these two senses together, as one is subordinate to the other: so that to be born *anothen* signifies both

to.

[1] Mat. 5. 34.

[m] Ver. 4.

[n] 1 Pet. 1. 3, 2

[o] Ver. 3 ?. Jo 19. 11. Jam 1. 17. and 17.

to be born *from above,* that is spiritually, and from heaven; and also *again,* or the second time? since that being born, which is from above, or of the Spirit, is a second birth, as it follows the firft and natural birth, which is after the flesh. "*Except a man be born again,*" our Saviour calleth it a *birth or being born,* to denote the *univerfal* amendment or renovation of man thereby: he intimates the neceffity of a renovation, not of this or that particular part or faculty, but a total renovation of the whole man, which is a new or fecond birth, whereby he becomes a *new man,* a *new creature,* and walks in *newnefs of life.* [P] Of which more under the *doctrinal* part.

[P] 2 Cor. 5. 17.
Gal. 6. 15.
Rev. 21. 5.

(2) The *origin* of *regeneration,* " *of water and the fpirit.*" The particle *ek* rendered *of,* as is plain from the fubject, denotes in this place, not the *material,* but the *efficient* caufe, as it doth in many other places; [q] since neither water nor fpirit are the matter out of which a fpiritual regeneration is effected. *Water and fpirit,* fome confider as two different things; fo that by *water* they underftand the *inftrumental,* and by *fpirit,* the *principal* caufe, becaufe (as they fuppofe) the fpirit, by water, effects regeneration. But they who are of this opinion are divided; fome by water underftand the Jewifh baptifms or wafhings, with which the Jews, more efpecially the Pharifees, were wont to wafh their profelytes, before their admiffion into the Jewifh church; likewife their own hands, clothes, meat and even their bodies, of which mention is made in various places of the new teftament; [r] to thefe, our Nicodemus, as he was a Pharifee, muft have been accuftomed. Others by *water* here, underftand the facramental water of *baptifm,* by which they fuppofe the Spirit effects regeneration. And here again fome fuppofe the baptifmal water to be *directly* intended, as moft of the Fathers; others, only by way of allufion. Others more rightly underftand but one thing expref-

[q] Rom. 11. 36.
Luke 1. 35.

[r] Mark 7. 8.
Heb. 9. 10.
Mark 7. 4.

fed,

fed by two terms, as the *water* of the Spirit, or fpiritual water, or rather the *Spirit* having the properties
of water, which like water cleanfeth in regeneration.
For our Saviour doth not mean to lead Nicodemus to
receive the facrament of baptifm, (which at that time
was not inftituted, at leaft as an ordinary, univerfal
facrament;) but to feek the regeneration of the Holy
Ghoft. "He faved us by the wafhing of regenerati- *Tit. 3. 5.
on :". wherefore in the continuation of this difcourfe,
our Saviour makes no further mention of water, but
only of the *Spirit.* I need not obferve that by *Spirit* t Ver. 6, 7,8.
here, is to be underftood the third perfon in the facred
Trinity, with relation to the work of fpiritual *purifica-*
tion, which is effected by regeneration and renovation. " *Tit. 3. 5.

(3) The *neceffity* of this regeneration, with regard
to which, may be obferved,

[1] The *manner* in which both the neceffity, and
univerfality of it are expreffed, *"except a man be born."*
A man, that is, every man, which extends the neceffity
to all and *every one,* fo that not one individual can be
excepted from this neceffity. However lefs is expreffed by this form of fpeech, than is intended. It
means not only that *no one* can be faved without this
regeneration ; but that *all* the regenerate fhall be fav-
ved. Not that regeneration (at leaft in it's limited
fenfe) is the only thing required unto falvation; fince
befides this, *converfion,* fanctification, &c. are neceffary,
in which the *power,* beftowed in regeneration, may be
drawn forth into the actual exercifes of faith and repentance : but that all and every one, who is regenerated, will alfo be brought to *converfion,* fanctification, faith and repentance, and fo to falvation.

[2] *The ufe,* or the purpofe to which regeneration is
fubfervient, viz. *"entering into the kingaom of God."*
The *kingdom* of God here fignifies both the kingdom of

thereof ; and alſo the kingdom of *glory* in heaven ; ˣ with all things which pertain to both theſe kingdoms, ˣ i. e. all ſpiritual bleſſings.

[3] The *poſſeſſion* and enjoyment of this kingdom. "*He cannot enter thereinto.* Ver. 3. "*He cannot ſee the kingdom of God.*" Here regeneration is extended to the *power,* "*he cannot,*" the reaſon of which is given in the following verſe, "*That, which is born of the fleſh,* that is by *natural* generation, is *fleſh,* or carnal, defiled with ſin ; and that, which is *born* of the *ſpirit,* is *ſpirit,* or *ſpiritual* and ſaving. For regeneration, ſtrictly ſo cal-

*Eph.2. 2. 5. ed, finds man ſpiritually *dead,* ᵃ into whom it infuſeth the firſt act, or principle of the ſpiritual *life*; by which he hath a *power* or ability to perform ſpiritual exerciſes. Therefore, without this, he *can* neither *ſee* the kingdom of God, that is *mentally,* as he is blind, "*He perceiveth not the things of the ſpirit of God : for they are fooliſhneſs unto him, neither can he know them, becauſe they

ᵇ 1 Cor.2 14. are ſpiritually diſcerned.*" ᵇ Nor if he could *ſee,* could he enter into the kingdom of God, as "*he is not ſubject to

ˣ Rom. 8. 7. the law of God,*" neither indeed *can be* ; ᶜ who alſo "*of

ᵈ 2 Cor. 3. 5. himſelf is not ſufficient to think any thing ſpiritually good.*" ᵈ Who therefore ſtands in abſolute need of *illumination* by regeneration, in order to his *ſeeing* the kingdom of heaven, and of a *renovation* of his will, in order to his willing to *enter* into it. Which power is afterwards excited in the exerciſes of faith and repentance, in converſion and ſanctification, whereby he *ſees* the kingdom of God, and at the ſame time *enters* into the ſame.

THE DOCTRINAL PART.

That beſides
the external
call, regene-
ration is alſo
neceſſary to
the applicati-
on of redemp-
tion, which is
proved by the
ſcriptures.
III. It is not ſufficient to the application of redemption, or a participation therein, that the Redeemer and the redemption purchaſed by him, be offered, by the external call of the goſpel, to thoſe who are to be ſaved, for their reception, unleſs that power be beſtowed upon them, by regeneration, by which they

one, without regeneration, *can* either *see* spiritual objects, or approach them, by entering into the kingdom of God. Hence faith, by which alone Christ is applied to us, and we made partakers of his redemption, is ascribed only to those who are *born of God.* [e] And the apostle is even more express than this, who, after that he had taught that the *kindness of God our Saviour had appeared unto men,* viz. By the external call of the gospel, adds, that he saved them, that is applied to them the *kindness* or redemption of the Savior, by the washing of *regeneration,* and the *renewing of the Holy Ghost.* [f] The same thing is held forth in all those texts of scripture, which ascribe our partaking of Christ's redemption; or our salvation, (1) In express terms to *regeneration,* and the renewing of the Holy Ghost : [g] (2) To *circumcision of the heart :* [h] (3) to the taking away of the heart of stone, and the *putting* within us a heart of flesh, the giving of a *new* heart and a new spirit. [i] (4) To the creation of a *pure* heart. (5) To spiritual *drawing* ; [l] unless you would choose to refer that to the grace of conversion. (6) To the *illumination* of the mind, [m] and *renewing* of the will. [n] (7) To a spiritual *resurrection* and *quickening.* [o] All which expressions are synonimous with regeneration, signifying the same thing in different terms.

IV. The foundation of this necessity lieth in the universal, *spiritual death* of all the elect, by which they, as well as reprobates, are by nature *dead* in sin ; [p] have an heart of *stone* ; [q] an *uncircumcised* heart ; [r] are blind in their *minds* ; [s] have their *wills* alienated from God, from the life of God, and from all spiritual and saving good ; [t] and are therefore utterly insufficient to think even the least good thought ; [u] and consequently also to receive, by a living faith, the Redeemer offered to them in the gospel, and the necessary terms of salvation ;

[e] John 1. 12, 13

[f] Tit. 3. 4, 5.
[g] James 1. 18.
1 Pet. 1. 3. 23.
[h] Deut. 30. 6.
Rom. 2. 29.
Col. 2. 11. 13.
[i] Ezek. 6. 26.
and Eze. 3. 19.
[l] 11. 19.
Jer. 32. 39. &
31. 32. [k] Psl. 51.
12. Eph. 2. 10.
and 4. 24.
2 Cor. 5. 17.
[l] Cant. 2. 3.
[n] John 6 44. 65.
[m] Eph. 1. 18.
[n] Phil. 2. 13.
[o] Eph. 2. 5. 6.
John 5. 25.
And by reason.
[p] Eph. 2. 1. 5.
& v. 14. Luke
15. 24. Mat. 8.
22 Ez. 37. 2, 3. 4
[q] Ezek. 36 26.
[r] Acts 7. 51.
[s] 1 Cor. 2. 14.
Eph. 4. 17, 18.
[t] Eph. 4. 18, 19
[u] 2 Cor. 3. 5.
Josh. 24. 19.

tion; unless, by regeneration, *power* be bestowed upon them in a new spiritual *life* by the Holy Ghost.
However a man spiritually dead can *hear* spiritual
truths; he can also, *grammatically* at least, *understand*
what he hears; he can moreover approve in his judgment, at least *speculatively*, what he understands, and
lastly he can in a general manner have some kind of
affection towards what he approves. Nor doth the holy
Spirit in the work of regeneration and spiritual quickening, treat with the elect, as with *stocks* or brutes;
but as *rational* creatures, to whose reception, the Redeemer, with the terms of salvation, have been already offered by the external call ; to the reception of
which, the Spirit hath *invited* them by the most pref-
sing motives. Yea it is possible that persons, as yet
spiritually dead, may, if not by the powers which they
are *naturally* poffeffed of ; yet by the affiftance of common grace, arrive to certain attainments, not accom-
panying falvation; [*] or that are not infeparably connected therewith. So that we are not to think, there
is nothing to be done with the unregenerate. However, while they perform *all* thefe things, they do *nothing* at all, which is *fpiritual*, or befure nothing in a
fpiritual manner. ^z

* Heb. 6. 4. 5.
6. 9.

z 1 Cor. 2. 13,
14.

**The meaning
of the word
regeneration.**

V. That we may attain to a more clear understanding of the *nature* of this regeneration, fo neceffary to
falvation : we muft carefully obferve with regard to
the *word*, that both the fcriptures, and also divines
ufe it, fometimes in a *larger* fenfe, to denote the *whole*
operation of the Holy Ghoft upon the fouls of thofe
who are to be faved; whereby they are brought into
a ftate of grace ; fo that, befides the external call, it
comprehends converfion, and even initial fanctification : In which fenfe practical divines lay down the
marks, motives, and means of regeneration : Sometimes the word regeneration is ufed in a more *limited*
fenfe, as diftinguifhed from the external call, from
                                                    converfion,

fication, at leaft in the order of nature, if not of time. It is in this *ftriƈter* fenfe of the word, we fhall confider the doƈtrine of regeneration at prefent. In which Expreffions fynonimous with regeneration. fenfe it means the fame with *circumcifion* of the heart, with *taking away* the heart of *ftone*, and *putting* within us a heart of *flefh*, with a new *creation*, with *drawing*, with *illumination*, with *turning* the will, and efpecially with a fpiritual *refurreƈtion* and *quickening*, of which we have already fpoken in feƈt. III. The terms ufed in Greek for regeneration are, *anakainofis*,[a] *agiafmos pneumatos*, [b]*kainee ktifis*, [c] *paliggenefia*, [d] *anageneefis*. [e] Thus regeneration, in the proper fenfe of the word, is only a *fecond* and fpiritual *generation*, in which the *foul* receives its *fpiritual life*, as the body receives it's *natural life* from the firft generation. The *father* in this cafe is God; hence we are faid to be *born* of God, [f] and the regenerate are called the *fons of God*. [g] The *mother* in whofe womb as it were we are conceived and nourifhed, is the church.[h] The *feed, the word of God, which liveth and abideth forever*; [i] received by the external call of the golpel. From all which confiderations, fince a *divine nature* is communicated to the regenerate, fimilar in its kind to the holinefs of the Deity, it is with fufficient propriety called a generation, as that is only a communication of life, with a refemblance to the Father begetting.

[a] 1 Tim. 3 5.
[b] 2 Thef 2 13
[c] 2 Cor. 5. 17.
[d] Mat. 19. 28.
[e] 1 Pet. 1. 3 2 2,
[f] John 1. 1.
[g] 1 Joh. 5. 1.
[h] Gal. 4. 26.
[i] 1 Pet. 1. 23.

C.   VI.

What the thing is, intended by regeneration.

VI. As to the *thing* intended by regeneration ; it is only that *phyfical* † operation of the Holy Ghoft, whereby he begets in men who are elected, redeemed and

† The word, *phyfical,* which is frequently ufed by our author, is offenfive to fome gentlemen, who feem not to reject the thing intended by it : their diflike thereto feems to arife from an apprehenfion that it implies the beftowment of a new natural faculty fuch as the underftanding, will, or affections : but this 'tis evident is not our author's meaning, and perhaps not the meaning of any, who ufe the term. They do not fuppofe the regenerate to exercife any natural faculty which the unregenerate do not. They ufe the word fimply in oppofition to *moral:* Now a *moral* operation is the effecting of fomething by moral fuafion or by the laying of arguments and inducements before the mind : but thefe, however great and ftrong, attended with never fo much light in the underftanding, our author fuppofes, will not effect this operation : but fuppofes there is a pofitive, immediate act of the divine fpirit upon the foul, infuling a new principle of fpiritual and divine life ; whereby the foul is enabled, or qualified to exercife its natural powers and faculties in a fpiritual manner. Some have chofen to exprefs themfelves hereupon in this form, viz. That God in regeneration acts after the *manner* of a phyfical caufe, as Dr. Ames, Rutherford, &c. and the fame thing, I take it, is intended by our Englifh Divines when they call that operation, which regenerates, *fupernatural.* They certainly ufe this word in oppofition to *moral,* or any operation by moral fuafion, or the laying of arguments and motives before the mind. See extracts from Ridgly, Willard, &c. in the appendix .---Indeed, 'till of late, fcarce any, but Pelagians, denied what is intended by a phyfical operation in regeneration, and the word *phyfical* has generally been made ufe of : tho' fome have reftricted the phyfical operation of the fpirit in regeneration to the underftanding, as moft of the *Arminians,* and fome of the *reformed,* who have held to regeneration by an illumination of the underftanding ; they feem to have been influenced to this reftriction, thro' fear, leaft, if they extended the *phyfical* operation to the *will,* the freedom of man's-will could not be maintained. But, tho' the generality of the reformed call the regenerating act of God a phyfical operation ; yet I no where find, that they call the *change,* that is wrought in man thereby, a *phyfical change.* The immediate term or effect of regeneration according to Van Maftricht is, (§ x. xi. xii.) *grace,* fpiritual life, &c. which is a moral change in the man, or a change of the moral ftate of his mind ; tho' wrought by a phyfical operation Nor is there any thing abfurd in this, that the operation fhould be *phyfical;* and yet the effect *moral:* for none would fuppofe it beyond the power of God, (if he is pleafed to exercife

and externally called, the *first act* or the principle of spiritual life, by which they are enabled to receive the offered Redeemer, and comply with the conditions of salvation. From this description may come into consideration,

VII. First. The *Author* of regeneration, which is God absolutely considered; [k] that *Father of Lights*, from whom cometh down every *good and perfect gift*; [l] because regeneration is a transient act, common to the whole Trinity; hence in the œconomy of redemption, it is attributed, (1) To the Father, as most agreeable to the character of a *father* which he sustains, *from whom all the family in heaven and earth is named*, [m][n] who therefore as he begat his *own* Son, so he also begets us; so that he is both his and our Father. [o] Again,

The Author of regeneration.
k John 1. 13.
Eph. 2. 5.
l Jam. 1. 17, 18
m 1 Pet 1. 3.
n Jam 1. 17, 18.
n Eph. 3. 15.
o John 20. 17.

ercise it) to determine the will of man to some particular volition, otherwise, than by arguments or motives; (this is before a possible case) here the operation would be *physical*, and yet the effect *moral*. So that the supposition of a *physical* operation, and yet a *moral* change as the effect of it, is not inconsistent in itself. And that this is actually the case, we trust our author hath sufficiently proved The word *principle*, which is here used for the immediate effect of this physical operation, and which is frequently used in this translation, has likewise given offence to some, as being a thing entirely unintelligible, a strange *something*, or a sort of *substratum* in the soul, which lies beyond the reach of human knowledge. 'Tis confessed it cannot be explained otherwise than by its consequences or effects. And is not the soul an *unknown* substratum of cogitation, whose existence can be known only by its operations? and what are the *faculties* of the soul, the *understanding*, *will* and *affections*, but *unknown* substrata of their several exercises? and what is matter but an *unknown* substratum of extension, solidity, &c. and what are all habits, but unknown substrata of their exercises? these substrata are unknown as to the nature of them. Their existence is known only by the qualities or actions they support. But who will disbelieve their existence, because they cannot fully comprehend the abstract nature of them? the implantation of a principle or substratum of holy exercises in regeneration is argued and known from its exercises, and operations. And we can tell the nature of it, as well as we can the nature of matter, of the soul, the faculties of the soul, and the like. And when these latter are explained, we shall think ourselves obliged to explain the former, or disbelieve its existence; but not before.

p 1 Pet. 1,2,3.
q 1 Cor. 15. 45
r Gal. 2. 20 compared with Phil. 1. 21. Col. 3. 4.
John 14 6
s John 3 3 5. Tit 3 5.
t Rom 8 2 10.
u Eph. 2. 5, 6.
w 1 Pet 1. 2, 3. Tit. 3. 5.
x Jam. 1 17.
a Eph. 2 1, 5.

gain, (2) Regeneration is afcribed to the *Son*, as the *meritorious* caufe ; who for this reafon is ftiled a *quick-ening fpirit*, and the life, which we live, we are faid to *live* by the faith of the *Son* of God. And (3) To the Holy Ghoft ; hence he is ftiled the *fpirit of life* ; becaufe the Holy Spirit by his operation *immediately* effects regeneration : and the fpiritual life is with peculiar propriety afcribed to the *fpirit of life.* The *moving* caufe is merely God's *great love,* his *abundant mercy ;* his gracious *good pleafure.* Nor is there, efpecially before regeneration, (while we are the children of *wrath, dead* in fin) any thing in us which can in the leaft merit fuch a favour. The *inftrument* of regeneration, (but that merely of a *moral* kind) is the word of God, previoufly offered and received in the external call of the gofpel, as we have already obferved.

b 1 Pet. 1.23.

VIII. *Secondly,* we may confider the *fubjects* of regeneration, which are, (1) *Men,* who are endowed with underftanding and will, to whom, agreeably to their *rational* nature, the Spirit hath previoufly *offered* redemption for their reception ; with whom therefore he is pleafed to treat, not as with ftocks or brutes, as we have already obferved. (2) They are the *elect* ; for regeneration is not a common gift ; but a gift proceeding from the moft *diftinguifhing* or fpecial grace, as it flows from God's *great* love, from his *abundant* mercy. (3) They are *redeemed* ; hence Peter fpeaks of regeneration, as peculiar to thofe, who are *fprinkled with the blood of Chrift.* Again, (4) They are fuch, who are as yet *dead in fin* : for unlefs a man be dead, he cannot be made alive by regeneration. I add, (5) The *whole* man throughout, is the fubject of regeneration ; the underftanding, will, affections, fenfitive faculties, &c. that all may be quickened and renewed thereby. As by natural generation, *all* the parts of a man are quickened or made alive ; and as, by fin, the *whole* man is become corrupt and dead.

The fubjects of regeneration.

c 1 Pet 1.2,3. & chap. 2. 9.
u Eph. 2. 5.
d 1 Pet. 1. 2,3.
e 1 Pet. 1 2,3.
f Eph. 2 1.5,6
g 1 Thef. 5 23.
h 2 Cor. 5. 7.
i Ifa. 1. 5. 6.

IX.

IX. *Thirdly*, we may confider regeneration itfelf, or
the regenerating *act*. Which certainly is not a moral
act, exercifed in offering and inviting, as is the cafe
with the *external call*. But it is a *phyfical* act powerfully infufing fpiritual life into the foul : Which is
proved, not only, (1) By the conftant phrafeology of
the *fcriptures*, when they fpeak of the *exceeding greatnefs
of his power towards thofe who believe, according to the
working of his mighty power,* or the *energy* of the power
of his might; yea the fame power which was exerted
in raifing *Chrift* from the dead. [k] Which expreffions
certainly do not befpeak a *moral* agency. Alfo where
the fcriptures fpeak of fpiritual *circumcifion*, of taking
away the heart of ftone, of putting within us a heart
of flefh, of creating a new heart, of drawing, of working in us to will and to do, of a *refurrection* from the
dead, of which we have fpoken in fect. III. Do thefe
expreffions in the leaft favour an operation merely
moral? But, (2) It may alfo be proved by the very
nature of the thing, in as much as regeneration is an
operation upon men fpiritually *dead*, infufing life into
them; [l] but what moral operation, in teaching offering, perfuading, can be rationally exercifed upon a
man that is *dead?*

X. The *term* of this phyfical operation, or the firft
and immediate *effect* of regeneration, is varioufly expreffed in fcripture. *Firft*, it is fometimes called *grace*,[m]
as *I will pour out the fpirit of grace* ; i. e. I will pour
out *grace* by my Spirit. *Be thou ftrong in the grace that
is in Chrift Jefus* ;[n] and in other places to the like purpofe. By which *grace* we do not here underftand,(1)The
free *kindnefs* of God, which is called *grace freely giving*
(*gratia gratis dans*) and external grace ; from which
not only *man*, but every *creature*, receiveth whatever
good he poffeffeth. By which alfo a man already regenerate, and poffeffed of fpiritual power, thro' a gracious providental influence, is excited to exert in *fpi-*
ritual

The act of
regeneration.

[k] Eph. 1. 19,
20.

[l] Eph. 2. 1. 5. 6.

The term or
immediate
effect of re-
generation.
1. Grace.
[m] Zach. 12. 10

[n] 2 Tim. 2. 1.
Heb. 13. 9.
1 Pet. 2. 19.

ritual operations, the power he hath received. But,
(2) By grace we here underſtand the *effect* of this kindneſs *grace, freely. given, (gratia gratis data)* . or *internal*
grace, which in the ſcriptures is called *chariſma,* [e] (the
free gift.) ·Nor, (3) Do we underſtand by grace here
every effect of this kindneſs, ſince all the good which
every creature enjoyeth, and even the whole creation,
is from the *grace* of God, and in this ſenſe univerſal grace
may be allowed : But we underſtand that grace which
is contradiſtinguiſhed to *nature,* and as it exiſts in man,
to the natural powers of *free will.* Neither, (4) Do
we underſtand hereby *every* effect of grace, by which
one man in his kind excells another. *v. g.* The gift
of mechanical *ſkill,* [p] or wiſdom in civil government,
which may be called *common* grace, by the aſſiſtance of
which, in things of a *moral* nature, a man may perform
any of thoſe things which are not (as the apoſtle ſays)
echomena ſoterias, or that have not a neceſſary connection with eternal ſalvation : But, (5) By *grace,* we here
underſtand that effect of God's kindneſs, or the chariſma (free gift) by which one man hath power to
perform ſpiritual exerciſes, while another hath it
not ; and ſuch exerciſes, indeed to which God
hath promiſed eternal ſalvation; which to uſe the
apoſtle's words, do accompany ſalvation (echomena
ſoterias.[q]) Finally in this ſenſe, by the grace beſtowed in regeneration, we underſtand that ſupernatural *power,* by which a man is enabled to comply
with the conditions of the covenant of grace, to
apprehend the Redeemer by a living *faith,* to come
up to the terms of ſalvation, to repent of ſin, to love
God and the Mediator ſupremely, &c.

XI. *Secondly,* the term or immediate effect of regeneration, is more frequently called *ſpirit.* [r] *That which
is born of the fleſh, is fleſh, and that which is born of the
ſpirit, is ſpirit;* [s] from which the regenerate are ſtiled
ſpiritual, [t] who are *ſpiritually minded;* [u] (phronema tou pneumatos,

[e] Rom. 12. 6.
& ch· 1. 11.
1 Cor. 1. 7.

[p] Exod. 31· 2. 3

[q] Heb. 6· 9.

[z] Spirit.
[r] John 3. 16.
[s] Gal 5. 16,
17 18. 22.
[t] Gal. 6. 1.
[u] Cor. 3. 1.
[x] Rom. 8. 7.

itos) who perceive the things of the spirit and spiritually ᵂ 1 Cor. 2. 14.
scern them. ᵂ By the word *spirit* here we underſtand
ɴot the Spirit *giving* ; but the *ſpirit given,* that is the
ſpirit, which the Holy Ghoſt beſtows in regeneration,
ᴛhe preſence of which makes the ſoul *ſpiritually* alive,
as much as the preſence of the animal ſpirit makes the
body *naturally* alive.ᵃ Hence this ſpirit is ſaid to quick-
ᴇn or make alive, ᵇ therefore it is ſtiled the ſpirit of ᵃ Ezek. 37. 5.
life, ᶜ becauſe the preſence of this ſpirit, which is *im-* Acts 20. 10.
planted in the ſoul, conſtitutes the *ſpiritual* life, and ᵇ John 6. 63.
capacitates and inclines the man to *ſpiritual* exerciſes, ᶜ Rom. 8. 2.
juſt as the natural ſpirit doth to *natural* exerciſes. This
ſpirit, beſtowed by the Holy Ghoſt in regeneration,
is, according to it's various exerciſes, ſtiled ſometimes
the *ſpirit of grace,* ſometimes the *ſpirit of prayer,* ᵈ the ᵈZach. 12. 10.
ſpirit of faith, ᵉ &c. agreeably to that virtue and ope- ᵉ2Cor. 4. 13.
ration which it produces in the regenerate. So that compared
by the ſpirit here we underſtand only that *ſpiritual* with Iſaiah
power, by which we are enabled to perform *ſpiritual* 11. 1, 2.
exerciſes in a ſpiritual *manner.* By *ſpiritual* exerciſes
or ſpiritual things we mean the ſame as the apoſtle by ᶠ 1 Cor. 2 14.
the things of the ſpirit, ᶠ and our Saviour, by *the buſineſs* ᵍ Luke 2. 49.
or the things of his Father. ᵍ

XII. *Thirdly,* the term, or immediate effect of re- 3. Life.
generation, is more clearly called ſpiritual *life,* in it's
firſt act (or principle,) from which God is ſaid to *quick-*
en, together with Chriſt, thoſe who are dead in ſin, ʰ ʰ Eph. 2. 5.
that we may be *raiſed* together with him in a ſpiritual
manner.ⁱ From the want of which ſpiritual life, the ⁱ Col. 3. 1.
unregenerate are ſaid to be *dead* in ſin, alienated from
the *life of God* ;ᵏ and from the preſence of which, on ᵏ Eph. 4. 18.
the other hand, we are ſaid *to live to God,* ˣ to the *will* ˣGal. 2. 20.
of God, and *according* to God. ˡ This ſpiritual life con- ˡ 1 Pet. 4. 2. 6,
ſiſteth in a *reunion* of the divine image, or original
righteouſneſs with our ſouls, by which our firſt parents,
in a ſtate of innocence, were enabled to *live* to God,
and were diſpoſed to all ſpiritual exerciſes.ᵐ For as ᵐ Eph. 4. 24.
the Col. 3. 10,

the *natural* life confifteth in the *union* of the foul with
the body ; fo the *fpiritual* life confifteth in the union
of original righteoufnefs with the foul. And as a man
hath power to perform all *natural* actions from the
natural life, fo from the ipiritual life the regenerate
have power to perform all *fpiritual* exercifes. And
laftly, as in the natural life, are virtually contained all
a man's *natural powers*, which afterwards, by organs
properly difpofed, come forth into action : fo in this
fpiritual life, are virtually contained all thofe *fpiritual*
graces, which, by the influence of converting grace,
are in due time drawn forth by degrees into actual
exercife.

4. The feed of God.
ᵍ 1 John 3. 9.

XIII. Hence *fourthly*, the immediate effect of regeneration is alfo called the *feed* of God. ᵍ Becaufe in the
grace, in the *fpirit*, and in the fpiritual *life*, which are
beftowed upon the elect in regeneration, are contained
the feeds of all thofe graces, which are neceffary to
falvation : Which, under proper circumftances, do,
by the heavenly dews of converting grace, gradually,
yet with abfolute certainty, in due time, put forth
their bloffoms and fruit in *actual* exercife ; like as the
feeds of vegetables buried in the earth, when watered
by genial fhowers, fhoot forth into the ftalk, flowers
and fruit. And, *fifthly*, this immediate effect is called

5. A new creature.
ʰ 2 Cor. 5. 7.
Gal. 6. 17.
ⁱ Eph. 2.
ᵏ Ezek 36.26.

a *new creature*, ʰ from which the regenerate are ftiled
the *workmanfhip* of God, *created in Chrift Jefus unto good
works, that they might walk in them.* ⁱ Alfo, *fixthly, it is*
called a *new heart* and a *new fpirit*, ᵏ becaufe thereby
the whole regenerate man, and all that is his, *fpirit* or

ˡ 2 Cor. 5. 17.
1 Thef. 5. 23.
ᵐ Eph. 4. 23.
24. Col. 3, 10.

underftanding, *heart* or will, all are *renewed*, ˡ from
which there is born a *new* man. ᵐ Thus far concerning
the general term, or the firft and immediate effect of
regeneration, which is the *fpiritual life* in its *firft* act (or
principle,) which is alfo called by other names, as
grace, the *fpirit*, the *feed of God*, a *new creature*, &c.

XIV.

XIV. This spiritual life, animating and quickening the *whole* regenerate man, and all the several parts and aculties of him, hath different *names* according to those ifferent faculties. As it takes place in the *understanding* it is called a *new spirit*, [n] and spiritual *light*, [o] and the bestowment of it by regeneration is called *illumination*, [p] and those who are illuminated are called *children of the light*; [q] are said to *walk in the light* of the Lord, [r] which light begets in them the *knowledge of the glory of God in the face of Christ Jesus our Lord*, [s] and also the saving *knowledge* of God, [t] and the Mediator. [u] This spiritual light of the regenerate effects, (1) The simple *understanding* or perception, [w] by which they know spiritual objects, not only speculatively as true, but practically as good. (2) It affects the *judgment*, so that the regenerate judge concerning the goodness of spiritual things, not only as to the general position (*in thesi*,) what is good in a general view; but also under all the particular circumstances and connections of that truth (*in hypothesi*,) what is good and profitable for them, at this very time, all circumstances considered. [x] In the mean time, this saving illumination in regeneration, is to be cautiously distinguished from the illumination, which is given in the external call, [z] in which spiritual light is rather held up to view, than conveyed [a] into the soul; or if some degree of light be bestowed by an internal work, [b] that however is either merely *speculative*, extorting only an acknowledgement, and profession of the truth, [c] or if it be practical also, is so only (*in thesi*) or representing only, in a general manner, the goodness of the truth acknowledged by him: [d] But not

Regeneration of the understanding, called illumination.

[n] Eph. 4. 23.
Rom. 12. 2.
[o] Eph. 5. 8.
[p] Eph. 1. 18.
2 Cor. 4. 6.
[q] Luke 16. 18.
Eph. 5. 8.
[r] 1 Thes. 5 5.
[s] Isa. 2 5
[s] 2 Cor. 4. 6.
Col. 3. 10.
[t] John 17. 3.
[u] Isa. 53. 2.
[w] 1 Cor. 2. 14.

[x] Ps. 73. 28.

[z] Heb. 6. 4.
[a] John 1. 5.
[b] Num. 24. 3. 4
[c] Mat. 7. 21. 22
Rom. 2. 17—23
[d] Mat. 13. 20, 21. Heb. 6. 4, [f] 2 Thes.

h Pſal. 51.12.

l Ezek. 36.25.

k Jer. 32. 39, 40. Heb. 8. 10.

i Ezek. 11. 19. 20.

m Rom. 2. 14. 15. n Luke 18. 10, 11, 12. Phil. 3. 5. 6. o Mark 10. 19, 20, 21. Heb. 6. 4, 5.

p Eph 2. 1. 5.

q 2 Cor. 3 5.

r Rom 7 22. 2 Theſ. 3. 5.

heart, h *a heart of fleſh,* or a heart eaſily affected, i a heart on which God hath *written his fear,* k by which the regenerate *walk in his ſtatutes.* l For the Holy Ghoſt implants in the heart or will, by regeneration, a new *inclination* or propenſity towards ſpiritual good. For altho' the will hath naturally a kind of propenſity toward *moral* good in general, m and toward *external* religious duties, n whereby, in duties, *with which ſalvation is not connected,* an unregenerate perſon may ſometimes perform things really wonderful : o Yet, their propenſity towards ſpiritual and *ſaving* good, mankind have utterly loſt by ſin ; hence they are ſaid to be *dead* in ſin, p and inſufficient to think even the leaſt thought ſpiritually good. q Wherefore it is abſolutely neceſſary, that a new *propenſity* toward *ſpiritual* good, be reſtored to the will. r For altho' the will doth naturally follow the *laſt* dictate of the practical underſtanding, ſo that, were the *underſtanding* but ſufficiently illuminated, an immediate renovation of the will might ſeem unneceſſary ; yet this is to be admitted for truth, only when the underſtanding, in its laſt dictate, judgeth agreeably to the *inclination* of the will. For that is *good,* with reference to the will, which is agreeable to its propenſity. So that, if we ſhould make the abſurd ſuppoſition of the *underſtanding's* being moſt clearly enlightened, and yet the *will* not renewed, the will would not follow the practical judgment, becauſe in that caſe the underſtanding would not dictate agreeably to it's propenſity. v. g. If David's underſtanding dictated, that chaſtity at this very time, all circumſtances conſidered, ought to be choſen by him, rather than adultery ; yet whilſt his underſtanding dictateth not agreeably to the preſent *propenſity* of his will, which inclineth to adultery, the will would by no means follow the laſt dictate of the underſtanding. It is therefore in this ſpiritual propenſity of the will, that the ſeeds of all thoſe graces, which are neceſſary

to

to falvation are contained : Hence the *feed* of the regenerate is faid to remain in them, by reafon of which they cannot *abandon* themfelves to fin, [a]

XVI. Nor is the *fpiritual life*, in regeneration, beftowed only upon the *fuperior* faculties of the foul, the underftanding and will : But alfo upon the *inferior* or fenfitive faculties ; the affections, fenfes, and even the members of the body. Hence the apoftle exprefly afcribes fanctification not only to *the fpirit*, by which he feems to underftand the fpiritual faculties, fuch as agree to fpirits only, as the underftanding and will : but alfo to the *foul*, (*Pfuche*, properly the animal foul, from which we are called *pfuchikoi*, natural or fenfual, as it is rendered,) which denotes the inferior faculties fuch as are common to brutes ; yea, he extends fanctification even to the body and members of the body. [t] For as by fin a fpiritual *death* and *irregularity* are bro't upon thefe faculties, whereby they ftrive againft the fpirit : [u] Which irregularity is exprefly reprefented as criminal by the Holy Spirit, (1) As it takes place in the *affections* or paffions of the foul, [x] (2) In the *fenfitive* faculties v. g. *feeing*, [w] and *hearing*, [a] (3) In the bodily *members*, [b] &c ; Therefore a fpiritual life, by regeneration, muft be reftored to thefe faculties, to enable them rightly to difcharge their refpective fervices. [c] This life in the *inferior* faculties is a *difpofition* to obedience, whereby they become fitted not to oppofe the fpirit, or underftanding and will, but to be in fubjection to, or to be led by the *fpirit*. [d] As at firft, in a ftate of integrity, by our original righteoufnefs, which confifted in the divine image, thofe inferior faculties were moft beautifully arranged under the government of the mind.

XVII. The fpiritual life is beftowed by regeneration, only in the *firft act* (or principle) not in the *fecond acts* (or operation,) underftood either as *habits* or *exercifes*. For as, by *natural* generation, a man receives

neither

[a] 1 John 3. 9.
Regeneration in the inferior faculties.

[t] 1 Thef. 5. 23.

[u] Gal. 5. 17.

[w] Rom. 5. 7.
Gal. 5. 24.
Col. 3. 5.
1 Thef. 4. 5.
Rom. 1. 26.
[x] 2 Pet. 2. 14.
[a] Pfal. 58. 5.
[b] Rom. 6. 19.
and 3. 13, 14, 15, 16.
[c] Rom. 6. 16.
[d] Gal. 5. 17, 18
Rom. 6. 12, 13 14. 17. Jam. 1. 20.

Regeneration confers the fpiritual life in the firft act only.

neither the habits or acts of reafoning, fpeaking, or writing, but only the *power*, which under proper circumftances, in due time, comes forth into act : So alfo, in regeneration, there is not beftowed upon the elect, any *faith*, hope, love, repentance, &c. either as to habit or act; but the *power* only of performing thefe exercifes, is beftowed ; by which, the regenerate perfon doth not as yet actually believe, or repent ; but only is *capacitated* thereto : Wherefore the unregenerate are emphatically faid, to be *unable*, either *to fee*, as referring to the underftanding, or *to enter*, referring to the will, into the kingdom of God. ᵉ Which power, in converfion, which fucceeds regeneration, proper circumftances being fuppofed, is, in due time, brought into *actual* exercife. So that one *truly* regenerate may, both as to habit and act, be for a time an unbeliever, deftitute of repentance and walking in fin. As appears, more clear than the light of the fun, in the inftances of thofe, who are regenerated in their mothers wombs, or at their baptifm, as Jeremiah, ᶠ John the baptift, ᵍ and Timothy, ʰ who neverthelefs did not, till they arrived to the years of difcretion, perform the actual exercifes of faith or repentance. So that *regeneration*, in which the fpiritual life is beftowed in the *firft* act or principle only, differs from converfion, by which this principle of life is brought into *actual* exercife, not only in order of *nature* ; but fometimes alfo in order of *time*. However we mean not to deny here, that it may be, and often is the cafe, that a fanctification of the fpirit, in a *general* fenfe, comprehending vocation, regeneration, converfion & fanctification properly fo called, is effected at one and the fame time : Which feems to have been the cafe with the thief on the crofs, converted by Chrift in his laft moments.ⁱ We only mean that they *may* be feperated as to time, and that oft times this is *actually* the cafe.

ᵉ John 3. 3. and 5.

ᶠ Jer. 1. 5.
ᵍ Luke 1. 15.
ʰ 2 Tim. 3. 15.

ⁱ Luke 23. 40. —44.

XVIII.

...ce therefore regeneration conveys the
, in the *first* act or principle ; it may be
mined. 1. That in regeneration a man is
ve, as in the first reception of a natural
ject of it can be only *merely passive*.[k] For
y thing toward begetting life in himself ;
already *alive*, since a dead person cannot
already *alive*, then surely life is not be-
m.

We may determine what ought to be
a *preparation* for regeneration : For there
nds of preparation come under considera-
one, which is supposed to proceed from the
regenerated, whereby, he prepares himself
egeneration ; or by the power of his own
becomes more disposed and prepared for
n than others. This, without the plainest
on, can by no means be admitted ; since
is an operation upon a man spiritually
whom the first act or principle of spiritual
d : Now, if he prepared himself thereto,
ly must do it by a previous principle of
must be supposed alive, before life is im-
im. The *other* kind of preparation is sup-
oceed from *God*, the author of regeneration.
this preparation, which is the work of
espect regeneration, either as taken in a
as denoting conversion also, and the term
e end of it, viz. Faith and actual repen-
which conversion terminates : That God
preparatory means to regeneration, taken
, by the help of which one may attain to
d repentance, we shall endeavour to shew,
assistance, in a *future* discourse : Or this
may respect regeneration in a more limit-

The affecti-
ons of rege-
neration. 1 A
man is en-
tirely passive
therein.
k John 1. 43,
with Eph. 2.
5, 6.

2. How far
regeneration
admits of any
preparation.

can any preparation, truly and properly so called, b'
admitted, any more than took place in the resurrecti
on of Lazarus to a natural life.[l] If, however, you
chuse to admit here *some kind* of preparation in those
who are to be made the subjects of this spiritual life
such, for instance, as in drying wood, which is to b
^l John 11.43. set on fire, such also as God used in the work of crea
tion, when he created on the first day a shapeless mass
which he formed and modified in the following days
and such as he peculiarly used in the creation of man
forming first the body of clay, or the rib, into which
^m Gen. 2. 7. he afterwards breathed *the breath of life.*[m] I say, if in
this sense you chuse, with many orthodox Divines, to
admit some *preparation,* which is the work of God,
have no great objection thereto : And then this pre
paration may consist in the previous external call, so
far as God, by the offers of grace, enlightens the mind
of the person, who is to be regenerated, concerning
the nature of redemption, and the terms of salvation
and invites him to embrace the same.

3. In what
sense regene-
ration is ir-
resistible.

XX. 3. We may hence determine, that regener
tion is *irresistible,* and in what sense this is to be u
derstood. For if you consider what the person, wh

ⁿ Acts 7. 51. is to be regenerated is, *a child of wrath, dead in sin ;*
^o Jo. 11, 43. 44 hath certainly depravity enough to resist :[n] But if y
^p Ezek. 36. 25. consider, that it is God, who regenerates and quicker
26, 27. Jer. the subject of regeneration can no more *resist* Go
32. 39, 40. than Lazarus of old *could* have resisted Christ, wh
compare Gal.
1. 13. Acts 9 raising him to a natural life.[o] Nor hath he *a will*
2—6, & 22. 5. resist, for, by the spiritual life instantaneously produ
with v. 10. & ed, all inclination or desire of resisting is suppressed
26. 9, 10. 14, taken away.[p]
with ver. 19.

4. In what
sense regene-
ration is in-
amissible.

XXI. 4. That the grace of regeneration, can nev
be *lost,* and the grounds upon which this *Inamissibi*

^q 1 John 3. 9. is founded.[q] In this indeed, it differs from the
Ezek. 36. 27. spiritual life, effected in creation, by the bestowm
[*] 11. 19 20. of original righteousness ; through the loss of wh
Jer. 32. 39, 40

sin, our first Parents became *spiritually dead*; since
e. spiritual life bestowed by regeneration is never
tirely lost. However, the unfailing permanency of
is life is by no means to be ascribed to the *firmness*
d constancy of the regenerate, or the *strength and
rfection* of the spiritual life; for there is, and always
wells, in the regenerate, so much corruption, that
iey are as likely, by their own conduct, to destroy
iis life, as our first parents were; and indeed more
), because they, before the loss of their spiritual life,
ere *perfectly* righteous and holy. But the impossi-
ility of loosing the grace of regeneration depends,
1) On the grace of election and of the divine purpose,
ence the gifts and calling of God are without repen-
ance. And, (2) Upon *preserving* grace.

XXII. 5. That this spiritual life, as conveyed in
egeneration, is but very *imperfect*, it being *only* the
irst act or principle of spiritual life, and only the *seeds*
of spiritual graces, which gradually like the seeds
of vegetables, grow up into the stalk, blossoms and
ruit. Hence the regenerate, merely as such, are stiled
iew born babes, *babes in Christ*, who still have need to
be nursed, and indeed with food suited to the infantile
tate: *That they may grow and wax strong in the spirit*,
is is said of John the baptist; that is, in order that
he *first* act or principle of life, conveyed in regeneration, might, by conversion, be drawn forth into actual
aith and repentance, which are the *second* acts or operations, and, if I may so say, the *branches* of this life:
And at length by *sanctification*, produce all these good
works, which are the fruits of the spirit. This spiritual life is indeed so small, that it cannot be well
known and distinguished, but by its growth and *exercises*; as *habits* cannot indeed be otherwise known,
than by their *Operations.*

THE ARGUMENTATIVE PART.

XXIII. The most of the controversies on this subject may, without much difficulty, be determined from

r Eph. 2. 1. 5.

s Eccl. 7. 29.
t Rom. 11. 29.
Math. 24. 22.
u 1 Pet. 1. 5.
John 10. 28, 29.
5. In what sense it is imperfect.

w 1 Pet. 2. 2.
x 1 Cor. 3. 1.
z Heb 5. 12.
13, 14.
o Luke 1. 80.

p Gal. 5. 22.

Q. 1. Whether regeneration consisteth in reformation of manners?

our *doctrinal* propositions. The *first* question upon
this subject is, Whether regeneration consisteth in a
reformation of *manners*? The rank Pelagians, as they
deny original sin, the loss of original righteousness,
and our being in a state of spiritual death ; and hold
only to *external* grace, which prescribes to man his
duty, and *excites* by arguments to the performance of
it : So they allow no regeneration, but what consisteth
in a reformation of manners, effected by the *external*
grace of God. The Socinians, those rankest Pelagians, tread in their steps, and affirm the same with them.
The Reformed consider a reformation of manners, as
belonging, not to regeneration, in its strict and proper
sense, but to conversion and sanctification ; while they
place regeneration solely in the reformation of the
inner man, the understanding, will, and other faculties, as we have shewn under the *doctrinal* part. Which
they support by the following reasons, (1) Man, by
breaking the covenant of works, hath lost his *original*
righteousness, in which the *spiritual* life of the soul consisteth, (and by the help of which alone our first parents were enabled to perform *spiritual* good, as we
have considered in a former discourse,) and so by sin
hath contracted *spiritual death*. (2) The scriptures expresly extend regeneration, to the renewing of the inner parts of the soul, to a *new heart*, a new spirit, to
the *writing* of the law upon the mind, and upon the
heart ; as in the *doctrinal* part. (3) A real reformation of *manners*, cannot result from any thing, but a
previous *principle of life*, and a renewing of the mind
and heart. Nor have our adversaries any thing to
urge in support of the contrary, but their own inconsistent suppositions, such as, (1) That the image of
God did not contain *original* righteousness, which we
have confuted in a former discourse. (2) That man
was not deprived of the image of God, so far as it
consisted in *original righteousness*, for transgressing the
law

2 Cor. 3. 5. 6.
1 Cor. 2. 14.
Rom. 8. 7.

Reasons of
our oppo-
nents.

law of paradife. Which we have already c
(3) That man did not by the lofs he fuftaine
tract fpiritual death. and univerfal impotence
tual and faving good, (which. hath been alrea
futed.) And therefore, (4) That there is
needs reformation in man but his *manners* (
conduct. The falfity of which naturally appe
what hath been already obferved.

XXIV. Queft. *Second.* Doth regenerati
from the free will of man, or from God alon
rank Pelagians, with whom the Socinians
agree, as they fuppofe that the nature and
of man were not impaired by the firft fin,
afcribe their regeneration, which they make t
in a reformation of manners, to free will alone
ing that they allow grace *externally* directing
fluencing in a way of *moral* fuafion ; yet fu
as may be *rejected* by the free will of man.
mi-Pelagians, with whom the Jefuits and A
agree, admit indeed, that the human nature
paired by fin ; that *blindnefs* was thereby brou
the underftanding, and a certain *debility (te*
the will : Therefore they hold to fome kind
grace, which may be excited, even as to tl
external grace in a way of moral fuafion ; b
may neverthelefs be *rejected* by the free wil
The Synergiftæ, among the Lutherans, w
Macrelius, in his ecclefiaftical hiftory, reck
rinus Strigelius ; hold that the *power*, whic
turally hath, may contribute *fomething* to
regeneration. The Lutherans in general h
man can, by the power of his *free will*, at
from pofitively *refifting* the Holy Spirit i
of regeneration, i. e. by the ufe of externa
may as it were open the door to the fpirit,
about to introduce the fpiritual life. The
altho' they allow, that after a fpiritual q

E

effected by regeneration, a man may, in conversion, co-operate with God unto the exercising of faith and repentance :ᶜ Yet, in regeneration strictly so called, they deny that a man can do any thing *actively* ; but affirm that he is *merely passive.* Because, (1) *Before* regeneration is effected, man is spiritually *dead* : therefore cannot, either in whole, or in part, contribute any thing towards begetting life in himself : for this contributing of something would suppose *life.* Because, (2) In regeneration there is bestowed a new *heart,* a new *spirit,* on which is written the law of God ; which certainly is to be ascribed to God alone. (3) There is in regeneration a *creation,*ˢ and a new *creature,*ᵗ which can be attributed only to God.ᵘ (4) *Of ourselves we* are insufficient to think even the least thought, with which *salvation* is connected.ʷ (5) God is said to work in us, *to will* according to his good pleasure.ˣ (6) The scriptures expresly declare, that it is not of him that *willeth,* or of him that *runneth* ; but of God that sheweth mercy.ᶻ (7) If man were, either in whole, or in part, the author of his own regeneration ; he would make himself to *differ,* contrary to the apostles assertion.ᵇ Nor doth what our adversaries allege, favour their opinion in the least ; as, (1) That we are sometimes commanded to *circumcise the foreskin* of our *hearts,*ᶜ to *make* to ourselves a *new heart, and a new spirit,*ᵈ to be *renewed in the spirit of our minds,*ᵉ and *to turn ourselves* to God.ᶠ To this I answer, (1) It is no ways inconsistent, that God should both *command* and *freely bestow* the same thing, according to the well known expression of Austin ; *da, quod jubes* (freely give what thou commandest)—thus God commandeth love ;ᵍ yet it is he, that shedeth it abroad in our hearts.ʰ (2) Those places of scripture, which are alleged, speak not of *regeneration,* strictly so called, by which God *infuseth* the first principle of life ; but of *conversion,* wherein he bringeth forth the life, already bestowed, into actual

tual

Marginal notes

r Cant. 1. 4.
Jer. 31. 18.
Reasons of the orthod ox opinion.

ˢ Pf. 51. 12.
ᵗ 2 Cor. 5 17.
ᵘ Isa. 45. 7.
ʷ 2 Cor. 3. 5.
ˣ Phil. 2. 13.

ᶻ Rom. 9. 16.

ᵇ 1 Cor. 1. 7.
Heterodox objections.
ᶜ Deut. 10. 16.
Jer. 4 4.
ᵈ Ezek. 18. 31.
ᵉ Rom. 12. 2.
ᶠ Joel 2. 13.
Mat. 4. 17.

ᵍ Mat. 22. 37.
ʰ Rom. 5 5.

tual exercife.[1] They object, (2) That if a man doth nothing towards his own regeneration, but is purely paffive, he is regenerated as a *ftock*, or ftone. To which I anfwer, this by no means follows, fince the fubject of regeneration hath been previoufly taught by the *external call* of the gofpel, and by *moral fuafion.* They object, 3. That to fuppofe a perfon doth not exercife a free felf-determining power as to his regeneration, would deftroy the freedom of the will. To which I anfwer, (1) A mans free will is no more concerned in his fpiritual *regeneration*, than in his natural *generation.* (2) Regeneration is not an *action* of the man, that it fhould be determined by his free will; but a mere *paffion*, in which he only admits (or is the object of) the action of God, being capable (as a rational creature) of having fuch an action performed upon him.

XXV. Queft. *Third.* Is the action of God, which regenerateth a man, *moral*, or *phyfical?* The rank Pelagians with the Socinians, as they place the nature of free will in *indifference*, and fuppofe alfo that the free will of man is unimpaired by fin, and therefore that a man, by his own *power*, can do whatfoever God requireth of him; allow nothing, but a moral *action* or agency of God in regeneration, in which, he *teacheth* what is to be done, and by motives perfuadeth to the doing of it. The Semi-Pelagians, together with the Jefuits and Arminians, as they acknowledge fome *internal* depravity as the effect of fin; fo they likewife allow fome *phyfical* agency of God in regeneration, which removes that depravity: But, as they reftrain the depravity, arifing from fin, to the *inferior* faculties of the foul, or at moft, to the underftanding; fo they allow the phyfical agency of God, only with refpect to thefe faculties: while, as to the *will* or free will of man, they hold only to a *moral* agency; yea, they fuppofe, that this *phyfical* action of God may be rejected

[1] Cant. 1. 4
Jer. 31. 18.
John 6. 44
65.

Q 3. whether the action of God, which regenerates, be moral or phyfical.

Different fentiments.

jected by the power of the will. The Reformed, altho'
they acknowledge a moral agency of God in the *external call* of the gospel, which is previous to regeneration ; and tho' they allow both a *physical* and *moral*
agency together in *conversion*, which follows regeneration : Yet in regeneration strictly so called, they admit
only a mere absolute *physical* agency. Because, (1)
Regeneration is the *first* implantation of the spiritual
life, before which, the person regenerated was spiritually *dead*.[i] Now moral *suasion* is no more sufficient,
or even conducive, to the begeting of the *spiritual*,
than it is, of the *natural* life. Because, (2) That spiritual *circumcision*[k]—*new creation*[l]—*taking away the heart
of stone*—*putting within us a heart of flesh*—*writing the
law thereupon*[m]—*and drawing,*[n] by which terms regeneration is expressed, is not a *moral*, but a purely *physical*
operation. Because, (3) *That superabundant greatness
of divine power*, which was exerted in the *raising* of
Christ from the dead, was not *moral*, but *physical* in the
highest sense : And the apostle testifies,[o] that the same
power is exerted in our regeneration. The principal
things, which can be urged upon the contrary side,
are, (1) That we read of God's bringing about regeneration by commanding it, (which, without doubt,
bespeaks a *moral* way of operation) as "*circumcise the
foreskin of your hearts*,[p] *make to yourselves a new heart*,[q]
work out your own salvation."[r] To which I answer. In
these commands God speaks to his *church*, to his people, who had long been his *delight* ;[s] therefore they
must have been already *regenerate* ; since, without regeneration, no one can see, or *enter into* the kingdom
of God.[t] Therefore, by these *commands*, God doth
not mean to bring about *regeneration*, as it denotes the
first infusion of the spiritual life ; but the drawing
forth of that life, which is infused by regeneration,
into the *second* acts or consequent exercises, (which is
expresly mentioned in the passage,[u] from whence the
first

firſt of theſe commands is quoted,) which is done in *converſion*, that follows upoh regeneration, in which man *being drawn runs after God ;* being turned, he actively converts and turns himſelf to God by the power of his grace.[x] It is objedted, (2) If regeneration is effedted by the *phyſical* agency of God alone, without any co-operation of the man, then man is regenerated as a *ſtock* or a ſtone. To which I anſwer, 1. Regeneration according to the ſcripture's, reſpedts man as ſpiritually *dead*,[a] as poſſeſſed of a *heart of ſtone*,[b] *unfit* for any *ſpiritual* exerciſes :[c] But is a man, that is ſpiritually dead, having an heart of ſtone, and being unqualified for vital operations, in any proper ſenſe, the ſame as a ſtock or a ſtone ? 2. Regeneration is wrought in man, after he hath been externally *called*, to whom grace hath been offered in a way of *moral* ſuaſion, and he invited to the reception of it ; thus, ſo far at leaſt, he is regenerated, not as a ſtock or a ſtone, but as a man. It is objedted, 3. That, by a *phyſical* regeneration, the liberty of the will would be impaired and even deſtroyed. To which I anſwer : Since by regeneration ſpiritual life is beſtowed upon the will of man, which was before dead, it is ſo far from being *deſtroyed*, that it is reſtored to its proper life and perfedtion.

XXVI. Queſt. *Fourth.* Doth the phyſical operation of regeneration affedt the *will immediately ?* The rank Pelagians, with the Socinians, allow no phyſical operation of God at all in regeneration ; but hold only to a moral and external operation. The Semi Pelagians, with the Jeſuits and Arminians, allow *ſome* phyſical efficiency in regeneration ; but ſuch as affedts not the *will*, or free will ; but only the *other* faculties of the ſoul. Some of the Reformed, v. g. John Cameron, and many others allow indeed a phyſical operation upon the *will* ; but that only by the *medium* of the underſtanding, which God, in regeneration, ſo

powerfully

w Cant. 1. 4.

x Jer. 31. 18.

a Eph. 2. 5.
b Ezek. 36.
25, 26, 27.
2 Cor. 3. 5.

Q. 4. Whether the phyſical operation of regeneration affedts the will immediately.

powerfully enlightens, and convinces, that the will cannot but follow it's laſt practical dictate. The ſynod of Dort, with moſt of the Reformed, extend the phyſical operation of regeneration to the will, and that *immediately,* as it begets in the will a new *propenſity* towards ſpiritual good, which, in my judgment, is moſt agreeable to truth. Becauſe, (1) The ſcriptures do, in expreſs terms, aſcribe the phyſical agency of regeneration to the *will,*[d] *it is God that worketh in us both to will,* &c. Becauſe, (2) In terms of the ſame meaning, the ſcriptures extend it to the *heart,* by which is always meant the will in ſcripture:[e] That God *creates* a new *heart,* and taking away the heart of ſtone, *puts* this new heart within us, and *writes* his law upon it : moſt certainly this is done by a *phyſical* operation. (3) The *will* is itſelf depraved by ſin, as well as the underſtanding, and inferior faculties ;[f] hence we frequently read of a *hard heart,* by reaſon of which, man is not *ſubject* to the law of God, neither indeed *can he be.*[g] (4) That corruption, which is ſeated in the *will,* would not be taken away by an illumination of the underſtanding : nor doth the will follow the laſt dictate of the practical underſtanding, unleſs it dictates agreeably to the *propenſity* of the will : v. g. if the will hath propenſity to *carnal* things, and the underſtanding ſhould judge, in the fulleſt manner, that ſpiritual thing at this very time, all circumſtances conſidered, were to be preferred ; yet the will would not follow : becauſe the will accounts that only as *good,* which is *agreeable* to its propenſity. Nor have they, who are of the contrary opinion, any thing to object here, except, (1) That upon this ſuppoſition the *freedom* of the will would be taken away. Which objection we have removed in ſolving the preceding queſtion. (2) That the will *always* follows the *laſt* dictate of the practical underſtanding ; therefore, were the underſtanding but powerfully enlightened, ſo as to judge that ſpiritual

thing

Reaſons for the affirmative.
[d] Phil. 2. 13.

[e] Pſal. 51. 12.
Ezek. 36. 25.
26. 27.

[f] Gen. 6. 5.
& 8. 21.
[g] Rom. 8. 7.

Objections in favour of the negative.

hings were better *for them*, than any senfual enjoy-
ments ; the will muſt neceſſarily follow : And therefore an immediate operation of God upon the will
ſeems unneceſſary, were the underſtanding but ſufficiently enlightened. To which I anſwer, (1) That
laſt *actual* dictate of the practical *underſtanding* doth not
take away that *habitual* corruption, which is in the
will. (2) That, upon the whole, is *good* to the will,
which is agreeable to its *inclination* ; wherefore, if the
practical judgment determine agreeably to this inclination of the will, the will always follows ; but if
contrary thereto, however powerful the dictates of the
underſtanding may be ; yet the will doth not obey.
It is therefore neceſſary, that in regeneration, a new
propenſity be infuſed into the will towards *ſpiritual*
good, that the practical underſtanding may dictate
agreeably thereto. *

XXVII.

* Preſident Edwards in his enquiry into the freedom of the will,
page 12. Boſton edition, obſerves thus, with regard to the will's
always following the laſt dictate of the underſtanding.

" It appears from theſe things, that in ſome ſenſe, *the will always follows the laſt dictate of the underſtanding*. But then the underſtanding muſt be taken in a large ſenſe, as including the whole
faculty of perception or apprehenſion, and not merely what is called *reaſon* or *judgment*. If by the dictate of the underſtanding is
meant what reaſon declares to be beſt or moſt for the perſon's happineſs, taking in the whole of his duration, it is not true that
the will always follows the laſt dictate of the underſtanding. Such
a dictate of reaſon is quite a different matter from things appear-
ing now moſt agreeable ; all things being put together, which pertain to the minds preſent perceptions, apprehenſions or ideas, in
any reſpect. Altho' that dictate of reaſon, when it takes place, is
one thing that is put into the ſcales, and is to be conſidered as a
thing that has concern in the compound influence which moves
and induces the will ; and is one thing that is to be conſidered
in eſtimating the degree of that appearance of good which the will
always follows, either as having its influence added to other things,
or ſubducted from them. When it concurs with other things, then
it's weight is added to them, as put into the ſame ſcale ; but when
it is againſt them, it is as a weight in the oppoſite ſcale, where it
reſiſts the influence of other things : yet it's reſiſtance is often o-
vercome by their greater weight, and ſo the act of the will is determined in oppoſition to it. "

Q. 5. Whether regeneration be irresistible or not. Different sentiments.

XXVII. Quest. *Fifth.* Is regeneratiou irresistible or not? The rank Pelagians and Socinians, as they allow only a *moral* operation of God in regeneration, and suppose the free will of man to be equally *indifferent*, either to receive, or to reject the divine influence ; hold it to be *resistible* : The Semi-Pelagians, with the Jesuits and Arminians, as they hold the regenerating operation to be *physical* in part, as it respects the understanding and inferior faculties ; and only *moral* in part, as it respects the will ; they maintain that it is in the *power* of the free will, so to resist the divine operation, that regeneration would by no means be effected. Some among the Reformed do not like the term *irresistible*, tho' they admit the term *insuperable.* We have allowed, in the *doctrinal* part, that the *moral* suasion of the *external* call, and also conversion, so far as it is effected by *moral* suasion, is *resistible* : But re-

Arguments of the orthodox.
a James 1.18.
h Rom. 9. 19.
i Phil 2. 13.
k John 10.29.
l John 6. 44. 65.

m Eph. 1. 19. 20.

n John 6. 37. with v. 44.
o Ezek. 11. 19. & 36.25, 26, 27.
p John 1. 13.
q Eph. 2. 5.

r John 11.43. 44.

generation we affirm to be absolutely *irresistible* ; for the following reasons, (1) Regeneration is effected by the *will* of God,[a] which the apostle Paul expresly asserts to be *irresistible.*[h] (2) God worketh in us both to *will* and to do,[i] and therein taketh away all *inclination to resist.* (3) By regeneration, the Father, who *is greater than all,*[k] *draweth* those who are regenerated.[l] And, (4) Draweth them *by the same exceeding greatness of power, by which he raised Jesus from the dead.*[m] (5) He so *draweth* in regeneration, that they, who are *drawn,* do infallibly *come.*[n] (6) By regeneration he taketh away the heart of *stone,* by which we make resistance to the divine call.[o] (7) God begetteth us by regeneration,[p] which act a man can no more resist, than he could his own *natural* generation. (8) By regeneration God *quickeneth,* or maketh alive,[q] which the subject of regeneration can no more resist, than a dead man can resist his being raised to a *natural* life, v. g. no more than Lazarus could resist Christ.[r] (9) If a man *could* resist, by reason of the *total* corruption of his nature,

nature,' he would continually do it.' (10) If he could — Rom. 7. 19.
refift, and yet did not actually refift ; he would have and 8, 7. Ifa.
of himfelf, the glory of not refifting, and of his own 1.5, 6.
regeneration ; and fo would make *himfelf* to differ, con- Acts 7. 51.
trary to the apoftle Paul's affertion." (11) If any one — 1 Cor. 4. 7.
could at his pleafure *refift* the divine agency in regeneration, then *all* could, and fo it might be the cafe,
that not one would be regenerated, and thus the whole
glorious defign of redemption might be *fruftrated*,
contrary to the apoftle Paul's affertion," and the gol- w 2 Tim. 2. 19.
den chain of predeftination be broken.ˣ   What our ˣ Rom. 8. 30.
adverfaries object here is of no weight at all, v. g. (1) Objections
They allege the words of Stephen, *Ye always refift the* of the hete-
*Holy Ghoft.*ᵃ To which I anfwer : They refifted the ᵃ Acts 7. 51.
Holy Ghoft, not when regenerating, but *externally*
calling, and that not indeed immediately ; but by men,
in a *moral* way, as plainly appears from the following
verfe, *Whom of the prophets have not your fathers perfecu-*
ted ? 2. They allege thefe words of our Saviour,
How often would I have gathered thy children together, &c.
*and ye would not ?*ᵇ To which I anfwer : By the ex- ᵇ Math. 23 37.
preffion, *I would have gathered you,* our Saviour doth
not mean, by the exertion of a *regenerating* power, but
by calling them in a way of *moral* fuafion, as the *pro-*
phets did, who were *fent* unto them for *this purpofe,*
whom they ftoned. 3. They object thele words from
the Pfalms, *O that my people had hearkened unto me, and*
*Ifrael had walked in my ways.*ᶜ To which I anfwer : ᶜ Pf. 81. 14.
The text plainly fpeaks of refiftance made not to regeneration ; but to the *external call :* as appears
from v. 9. to 12. They object, 4. What is faid in
Ifaiah, *What could I have done more to my vineyard, that*
*I have not done in it ?*ᵈ To which I anfwer: The prophet ᵈ Ifa. 5. 4.
is fpeaking, (1) of the benefits purchafed by Chrift

of *regeneration* which is *internal.* They object, 5.
That, upon this suppofition, no one *can* be regenerated, but thofe who actually are fo. To which I anfwer : With refpect to *man,* it is true, no one *can* be
regenerated, but he who actually is fo ; becaufe all
are dead in fin : but, with refpect to *God,* all things

Mat. 19.26 are poffible.* They object, 6. That upon this fcheme,
they who refift do the *will* of God. To which I anfwer : They refift the *preceptive* will of God, which
only prefcribes to rational creatures their duty ; but,
they do not refift the *decretive* will of God, which go-
verns the event.

Q. 6. Whe-
ther there be
any prepara-
tion to rege-
neration.

XXVIII. Queft. *Sixth.* Doth regeneration admit
of any *preparation ?* The Pelagians and Semi-Pelagians, with all their followers, the Socinians, Jefuits and
Arminians, maintain the affirmative ; becaufe they
hold that the efficacy of converting grace depends
upon the *free will* of man ; and fuppofe that *one* is by
nature more prepared for converting grace than *another* ; or that he can thus prepare himfelf by his own
power. The Reformed admit indeed of preparations
in regeneration, taken in a large fenfe, to fignify the
fame as converfion ; thus Perkins in his Cafes of Con-
fcience, Sect. I. Ch. v. vi. xi. Dr. Ames in his Caf.
Con. Lib. II. Ch. iv. How far preparations may be
admitted, and how far not, we have explained in the
doctrinal part, § XIX. viz. That regeneration, underftood to fignify only the *firft* implantation of the fpiritual life, admits of no preparations, excepting what
arifeth from the offers and moral invitations of the
external call of the gofpel ; if you chufe to call that a
preparation ; becaufe the firft implantation of the fpiritual life is effected in a moment, juft as a refurrection
to a natural life is ; nor can there be any middle ftate
between fpiritual life and fpiritual death.

Q. 7. Whether
regeneration
can be ever
wholly loft.

XXIX. Queft. *Seventh.* Can regeneration once
wrought ever be *wholly loft ?* The Pelagians, with all

the

the favourers of Pelagianifm, maintain the affirmative; becaufe they ftrenuoufly hold to fuch a *free will* in man, as can either diveft itfelf of grace received, or receive it at pleafûre, (with whom, in this point at leaft, the Lutherans agree; as they hold that one truly regenerate may totally fall from grace.) The Reformed hold it can never be wholly loft; but this they fuppofe to depend, not upon the power of the *regenerate*, but upon God's immutable decree of *election*, Reafons of the orthodox. and his almighty upholding power: which is evident from the following reafons, (1) The *feed* of the regenerate is faid to abide in them.[f] (2) It is faid of the f 1 John 3. 9. regenerate, in confequence of their being endowed with a heart of *flefh*, that they fhall walk in God's ftatutes,[g] *fhall keep* his judgments and do them. (3) It g Ezek. 36. 26, 27. is evident from the *infeperable* connection there is between predeftination and glorification.[h] (4) The *foundation of God ftandeth fure, having this feal, The Lord* h Rom. 8 30. *knoweth them that are his.*[i] (5) The *truth* of God ftands i 2 Tim. 2. 19. engaged for the perfeverence of the regenerate.[k] Nor k 1 Pet. 1. 3, 4, 5. John 10. 28, 29. doth it help our adverfaries to object, (1) That a righteous man may *turn* from his righteoufnefs.[l] For l Ezek. 3. 20, and 18. 24. Objections of the heterodox. I anfwer: The prophet is fpeaking here, [1] of a *natural* power (*de potentia caufæ*,) by which, even the truly righteous confidered in themfelves, can fall from grace; but, not of what will actually take place (*de potentia effectûs*) as tho' they, who are upheld by God, could fall away into total apoftacy. [2] The prophet fpeaks *conditionally*, if the righteous man fhould turn, he would die; and not *abfolutely*, that a truly righteous perfon can actually fall away. But, [3] The prophet doth not fpeak of the *truly* righteous, or thofe who are *internally* fo by regeneration, converfion and fanctification, who never can fall away;[m] but of thofe m Pf. 37. 1. 18. 20. 24 who were righteous in *appearance* only, or in their *own* 125. 1. 2. 3 eftimation.[l] (2) Our adverfaries infift upon there being inftances of thofe who have finally fallen away; l Math. 9. 3 with Luke 18. 9. 10.

as Judas, l Demas, m Hymeneus and Alexander: n To
which I anfwer, It remains to be proved that they
were ever truly regenerated; this text is exprefly a-
gainft it ; ° *Whofoever is born of God doth not commit fin,
for his feed remaineth in him, and he cannot fin; becaufe he
is born of God.* They object (3) That there are certainly inftances of the truly regenerate, who have fallen from grace, in the drunkennefs of Noah, the
adultery and murther of David, Peter's denying his
Lord, &c. To which I anfwer, They omitted, or rather neglected fome *fecond* acts or exercifes of the fpiritual life; but they never wholly loft the *firft* act or
principle, which was beftowed in regeneration. p They
object, (4) If the regenerate *cannot* lofe the grace of
regeneration, they would ceafe to be *free agents.* To
which I anfwer, The confequence by no means follows; fince the conftant prefence of the fpiritual life
in the will rather *confirms* the liberty of it.

XXX. Queft. *Eighth.* Whether regeneration be *univerfal,* or whether all men are regenerated ? *All* the
Papifts, as well the Dominicans, as the Jefuits, (as
they fuppofe *fufficient grace* given to every man, whereby he *can* be faved) do, in effect, hold regeneration to
be *univerfal,* (fince according to the fcriptures, in regeneration properly fo called, there is conferred only
a *power* to perform fpiritual good, as we have fhewn
under the *doctrinal* part.) However, in the explanati-
on of this fufficient grace, they greatly differ. The
Dominicans indeed fuppofe that *fufficient* grace is given to all ; but yet fuch as cannot put forth itfelf into
actual exercife, without *efficacious* grace preceeding:
But the Jefuits hold to fufficient grace, whofe *efficacy*
depends upon the free will of every man. The rank
Pelagians and Socinians, as they make regeneration to
confift in a *reformation of manners,* fuppofe finners have
by nature, that power, whereby they *can* regenerate
themfelves, or reform their moral conduct : But they
do

do not fuppofe that an *actual* reformation of manners takes place in every one ; but only in thofe, who *will* to reform their moral conduct. They exprefly exclude regeneration from *infants*, both on account of their having no inherent fin, and alfo on account of their incapacity, from the want of reafon, to reform their moral conduct. Among the Reformed who hold to *univerfal* grace, there are fome who fuppofe, that by the grace of God power is *reftored* to *all*, and every man, whereby they can be faved, if they *will* ; altho' there is given to the *elect* alone that power, by which they are actually made willing. The renowned Cocceius, altho' he doth not deny that regeneration took place under the old teftament ; yet in the emphatical fenfe of it, he confines it to new teftament times. The general opinion of the Reformed is, that the grace of regeneration is in the higheft fenfe peculiar to all the *elect*; and they fuppofe alfo that even *infants* are fometimes the fubjects of it, which they fupport by the following reafons, (1) The fcriptures, as often as they make mention of regeneration, extend it, not to *all* promifcuoufly ; but to the *elect* only,[q] and that, (2) To the *exclufion* of all others.[r] (3) The fcriptures exprefly declare, there are fome who have not this *power* which is conferred in regeneration.[s] Yea, (4) The fcriptures do extend regeneration particularly to *infants*.[t] Nor can any place of fcripture be produced by our adverfaries to the contrary, which teftifieth, either that regeneration, the fpiritual life, a power of performing fpiritual good, or fufficient grace is granted to all and *every* one.

XXXI. Queft. *Ninth.* Whether regeneration be *neceffarily connected* with baptifm ? The Socinians rightly deny it ; but upon a wrong hypothefis, that the baptifm of water is but an indifferent rite, introduced by the apoftles, without the command of Chrift, having no ufe or efficacy. The Anabaptifts likewife deny

The general opinion of the reformed with their reafons.
[q] 1 Pet. 1. 3.
Eph. 2. 3. 4. 5.
James 1. 18.
John 3. 3—8.
[r] John 6. 43, 44. 64. 65.
[s] Rom. 8. 7.
Jer. 13. 23.
[t] Jer. 1. 5.
Luke 1. 15.
2 Tim. 3. 15.

Q. 9. Whether regeneration be neceffarily connected with baptifm.

deny it, who allow no ufe or efficacy of baptifm, but that of *fignifying* the *church* covenant, and diftinguifhing thofe who are in *that covenant*, from thofe who are without. On the other hand, the Papifts, in order to maintain that the facraments of the new teftament beget grace *ex opere operato*, or of their own proper virtue; hold that the baptifm of water effects regeneration, hence they frequently ufe baptifm and regeneration to fignify the fame thing. The Lutherans do not indeed atribute any regenerating *efficacy* to the baptifmal water; however they fo confine the regenerating influences of the fpirit to baptifm, that they fuppofe no one can ordinarily be regenerated without it. The Reformed, tho' they unanimoufly hold that there is no *phyfical* regenerating efficacy in baptifm; but only a *moral* efficacy, which confifts in its being a *fign and feal* of regeneration; and alfo that the grace of regeneration is not confined to any facrament; and yet that baptifm is not a mere naked, ufelefs *fign*, but a moft efficacious *fealing* of the covenant of grace and of *regeneration*, to thofe who receive it agreeably to it's inftitution, and alfo to the *elect infants* of believers: yet as to the manner and time of it's becoming effectual they fomewhat differ. Indeed as to the baptifm of *adults*, that, if *rightly* adminiftered, doth, by the confent of all the orthodox, certainly prefuppofe regeneration as already effected; becaufe it exprefly requires faith of the fubject of baptifm, and fuch faith indeed as proceeds from the *whole heart*; [a] which cannot take place without a previous regeneration: for whatfoever is born of the flefh, is flefh; and whatfoever is born of the fpirit is fpirit. [b] But as to the baptifm of *infants*, here the orthodox are divided; fome deny that regeneration can *precede* baptifm, which therefore, as they fuppofe, only feals regeneration as *future*, when the elect infant fhall arrive to years of difcretion, fo as to be capable of faith and repentance; thus

[a] Acts 8. 36, 37

[b] John 3. 6.

thus the celebrated Amyraldus. But he inaccurately confounds *regeneration*, which beftows the fpiritual life in the *firft* act or principle, (by which the infant is effectually enabled; when he arrives to the exercife of reafon, to believe and repent,) with *converfion* ; which includes the *actual* exercifes of faith and repentance ; which cannot take place before the years of difcretion. Others, from modefty declining to determine the point, think it depends on the fovereign will of God, whether to beftow regeneration *before* baptifm, at the time of its adminiftration, or afterwards ; thus Zanchy in hisCommen. upon Eph. v. in a digreffion concerning baptifm ; and Ames in his Bellarminus enervatus Tom. III. XIV. Queft. III. Spanheim the father in his Dub. Evang. Part III. Dub. XXVII. Others chufe to think that regeneration is effected at the *very time* of baptifm, *ordinarily* at leaft : Thus Lewis Le Blanc, with the Papifts and Lutherans, who fuppofe this always to be the cafe, thus the celebrated Peter Jurieu, Beza, and others. The common opinion of the Reformed is, that the baptifm of infants (at leaft of the *elect*) prefuppofes regeneration as already effected ; becaufe that which is not, cannot be *fealed* by baptifm. And this opinion appears to me moft agreeable to truth. Befure baptifm itfelf doth not *effect* regeneration, as the Papifts fuppofe ; Nor are the regenerating influences of the Holy Spirit *confined* to external baptifm, as the Lutherans would have it. Becaufe, (1) The *efficacy* of baptifm confifts in it's *fealing*, agreeably to the nature of all facraments fo far as they are *feals* ;[c] which prefuppofes regeneration, as the prinple of faith. Becaufe, (2) The pollution of the foul is not purged away by the baptifm of water,[d] therefore regeneration is not confined thereto. And, (3) If this was the cafe, all the baptized would be regenerate, and that, at the very time of their baptifm : Againft which the fcriptures fpeak,[e] and alfo experience fhews,

The general opinion of the reformed, with their reafons,

[c] Rom. 4. 11.

[d] 1 Pet. 3. 21.

[e] Acts 8. 13. 20, 21, 23.

that

that many baptiz'd perfons live moſt abandoned lives, and are not finally ſaved. We read alſo of perfons regenerated *before* their baptiſm, as the Eunuch,[f] the Centurion and his family ;[g] yea, of thoſe who were *never* baptized at all, as the thief upon the croſs ;[h] according to the common obſervation, *that it is not the want of baptiſm, but the* contempt *of it that is damning.*

(4) Regeneration is limited to no ſacrament, not to *circumciſion,*[i] not to the *paſſover,*[a] not to the *Lord's ſupper,*[k] nor to any legal waſhings,[l] therefore not to baptiſm, ſince 'tis expreſly ſaid, that even a baptized perſon, if he believes not, ſhall be damned.[m] I will only add, (5) That the Holy Ghoſt is ſaid to regenerate according to his ſovereign pleaſure ; *as the wind bloweth where it liſteth, ſo is every one born of the Spirit.*[n] 'Tis however alleged in favour of the contrary ſide, (1) That Chriſt hath inſeperably connected regeneration with *water and the ſpirit.*[o] To which I anſwer : He doth not mean the external water of baptiſm, which at that time was not inſtituted as an ordinary and univerſal ſacrament of the new-teſtament ; but by *Hendiadis,* he means the water of the Spirit, or the Spirit cleanſing, like water, in the work of regeneration. In like manner it is ſaid, *he will baptize you with the Holy Ghoſt and with fire,*[p] i. e. with the Spirit, having the purifying quality of fire ; which our Saviour ſufficiently ſhews to be his meaning, when he aſcribes regeneration to the Spirit alone :[p] Compare herewith what hath been ſaid upon this point in the *explanatory* part. 'Tis alleged, (2) That the waſhing away of ſin,[q] regeneration, [r] and ſalvation [s] are aſcribed to baptiſm ; therefore baptiſm either works regeneration by it's own virtue, or at leaſt the Holy Spirit hath inſeperably connected his regenerating influences therewith. To which I anſwer : Neither of theſe is the caſe ; but only that the Holy Spirit, by baptiſm, ſealeth regeneration to the elect ; as we have already, obſerved.

[f] Acts 8. 36. 37.
[g] Acts 10. 2. 22. [h] Luke 23.

[i] Rom. 2. 25. 27, 28.
[a] 1 Cor. 10. 3. 4. [k] 1 Cor. 11. 27. [l] Heb. 9. 10 & ch 10 4.

[m] Mark 16 16.
[n] John 3. 8.
Objections.

[o] John 3. 3. 5.

[p] Mat. 3. 11.

[p] John 3. 6. 8.

[q] Acts 22. 16.
[r] Tit. 3. 5.
[s] 1 Pet. 3. 21.

obferved. (3) They argue on the other fide from this
text, *Know ye not, that fo many of us as were baptized
into Jefus Chrift, were baptized into his death?* To which * Rom. 6. 3.
I anfwer : This text means only. that all the elect,
being true believers, baptized according to inftitution,
have communion and participation in the death of
Chrift, which is fealed to them by baptifm : But it is
not faid that this communion is effected particularly
by baptifm, much lefs, that this communion is abfolutely connected with baptifm. 'Tis argued, (4) As
many as are baptized into Chrift, *put on Chrift,* confequently are regenerated. To which I anfwer : The * Gal. 3. 27.
text doth not fay that they *put on* Chrift by baptifm ;
but that they, who are baptized, had *before* put on
Chrift. Since therefore communion with Chrift,
which is fignified by the term of putting on Chrift,
hath been already effected in baptized perfons, 'tis not
effected by baptifm ; but being already effected, is
fealed by this facrament. (5) 'Tis argued by thofe of
the contrary opinion, that theirs is the received opinion of the fathers, and alfo of eminent men among
the Reformed themfelves, v. g. of Auftin and Profper
among the Fathers, of Pareus, Davenant, Ward and
Forbes among the Reformed. To which I anfwer :
The Fathers, whenever they fpeak of baptifm, are
wont to ufe very ftrong expreffions ; neverthelefs, they
very often fuppofe regeneration and faith as previous
to baptifm : Thus Juftin Martyr, reprefenting the
practice of the primitive church, faith, *"Whoever have
been perfuaded and have believed—and have received power
fo to live—are then brought by us to the water and are
REGENERATED, after the fame mode of regeneration, in
which we ourfelves have been regenerated."* The Fathers
therefore can by no means be reconciled with each
other, without a diftinction of regeneration into *real,*
which *precedes* baptifm, and *facramental* which confifts
in a folemn profeffion, declaration and fealing of that,

G which

which is *real.* In which sense the Reformed divines
also hold that regeneration is effected by baptism.

THE PRACTICAL PART.

Practical in-
struction.
XXXII. You will now, perhaps, reader, promise
yourself a very large application of this important
subject, since practical writers have so much exerted
themselves upon it. But, if I shall not fully answer
your expectations, you will consider these two things.
(1) Those practical writers treat the subject of regeneration in a *larger* sense, as comprehending the *whole*
internal operation of the Holy Spirit upon the redeemed, in which are contained vocation, spiritual
quickening, conversion and sanctification ; whilst we
have taken it in a *stricter* sense, as denoting only the
bestowment of the *first act* or principle of spiritual life :
Hence they bring under regeneration those things
which properly belong to conversion and sanctification.
If the reader is pleased to consider this subject in the
same latitude with them, he may, without much difficulty, apply here, what is said, by way of improve-
ment, under the heads of conversion and sanctification.
(2) It is to be considered here, that the *first* act of
life is conferred, only in order to the *second* acts, as
habits are only in order to their second acts or exercises ; nor can it be known or discerned, but by the

men can be *saved* ?ˣ For if you confider the fubject, who is to be made alive; he is fpiritually *dead*, dead in fin ;ᵃ *who feeing doth not fee, and hearing doth not hear, or underfland.*ᵇ If you confider the *work itfelf*, this is effected only by a fecond *generation*,ᶜ a *creation*,ᵈ *quickening*,ᵉ *taking away the heart of ftone, putting within us a heart of flefh, writing the law of God upon the heart*,ᶠ or by a *renovation* of the whole man.ᵍ If you confider the *manner* of operation, this requireth in the author of it, (1) *Infinite power, a fuperabundant greatnefs of power*, as great, and, if poffible, even greater, than was exerciled in creation : Becaufe there was not only no neceffity, in order to creation, of the *death* of the Son of God, as there is in the reftoring of a finner to life : But there was no *contrary* difpofition of the object, fuch as an heart of ftone, which knows not how to believe, fuperable by nothing fhort of *infinite ftrength* : As great a power alfo is neceffary, as was required to raife the dead.ⁱ (2) It requires in the author of regeneration, infinite or exhauftlefs *goodnefs* and mercy,ᵏ by which, that we may not all *perifh* eternally by the *firft* generation, he is pleafed to add a *fecond* : And left, by the *firft* life, we contract eternal death, he is pleafed to add the *fecond* : And that our fouls may not be dead in *living* bodies, he is pleafed to reftore to them the *fpiritual* life loft by fin. It requires, (3) Infinite, or the moft abfolute *fovereignty* ;ˡ hereby, paffing by whom he will, he beftows the fpiritual life on whom he *pleafes* : paffing by for the moft part, the more noble, and as it were the more *worthy*, he beftows it on the more *mean* and contemptible,ᵐ and of materials in themfelves fo *unfuitable*, he is pleafed to rear an edifice fo *magnificent*. As appears in the cafe of Zacheusⁿ — f Paul ° — of the harlots in preference to the reputable Pharifees.ᵖ Regeneration inculcates the greatnefs of the work of reftoring a finner to *life*, for thefe ends, (1) That we might more particularly acknowledge,

Margin notes:
ᵏ Mat. 19. 25.
ᵃEph. 2. 1. 5.
ᵇMat. 13. 13. 14. 15.
ᶜJohn 3. 3. 5.
ᵈPfalm 51. 12. Eph. 2. 10.
ᵉ Eph. 2. 5. 6.
ᶠ Ezek. 36. 25. 26.
ᵍ 2 Cor. 5. 17.
ʰ Eph. 1. 19. 20
ⁱ Eph. 1. 20.
ᵏ Eph. 2. 4. 5. and ch. 3. 8. 9.
ˡ Rom. 9. 15. 16. 18.
ᵐ 1 Cor. 1. 25. —29.
ⁿ Luke. 19. 7. 5. 8.
° 1. Tim. 1. 13. 14.
ᵖ Mat. 21. 31.

ledge, what great *obligations* we are under to God, that he hath regenerated and brought us into a ſtate of life, while ſo many thouſands are paſſed by, and that we might ſhew ourſelves more ready to make *grateful* re-

¹ Tim. 1. 13. turns.ᵃ (2) That, on account of the infinite power, goodneſs and benevolence, which God hath exhibited in our regeneration, we might be the more careful to

¹ Pet. 1. 3. live to his glory.ᶠ (3) That with regard to our future happineſs, we might more humbly depend upon his grace, and work out our ſalvation with *fear and trem-bling* ; becauſe it is God alone, who worketh in us both

Phil. 2. 13. *to will and to do.*ᵍ (4) That we might not, from our ſtate's being better than that of others, *exalt* ourſelves

Luke 18 11. above them ;ᵗ that we might not *boaſt,*ᵘ ſince it is God

Eph. 2. 5. alone, who, by regeneration, makes us to differ from the worſt of mankind ; and whatever good we have

¹ Cor. 4. 7. above them, we derive it wholly from him.ʷ (5) That we might not wonder if the moſt powerful ar-guments to converſion, uſed by men, have not always anſwerable ſucceſs ; ſince it is not *of Paul, that plant-eth, nor Apollos, that watereth, but of God, that giveth the*

¹ Cor. 3. 6 7. *increaſe* ;ˣ for the Spirit, in his regenerating influences,

ª John 3. 8. *bloweth where he liſteth* ;ᵃ and the *natural* man is natu-

ᵇ Eph. 2. 1. 5. rally *dead in ſin* ;ᵇ and the Father *draweth* not all pro-

ᶜ John 6. 44. miſcuouſly.ᶜ (6) That we might not readily deſpair
64. 65. of the converſion of *any one,* however great his oppo-

ᵈ 2 Tim 2. 25. ſition thereto may be ;ᵈ for the Spirit is *able* to rege-
26. nerate and quicken him, when it ſeemeth good in his ſight.

2. It recom-
mends to us
the bleſſed-
neſs of the
regenerate.   XXXIV. *Secondly.* This ſubject recommends to us the *happy* condition of thoſe, who, with ſo much dif-ficulty, have been brought, by regeneration, to a ſpi-ritual life : *Bleſſed be God—who hath begotten us to a lively*

ᵉ ¹ Pet. 1. 3. *hope*ᵉ—For, (1) they are *born not of fleſh,* nor *of the wil*

ᶠ John 1. 13. of man, but *of God.*ᶠ (2) They are made *alive* from the

ᵍ Luke 5. 22. dead.ᵍ (3) They are by way of eminence the *work-*

ʰ Ep. 2. 10. Pſ. *manſhip* of God ;ʰ in a peculiar manner produced by
100. 3. com-   him
pared with
deut. 32. 6.

him.[j] (4) They are *new creatures,*[k] in many respects more excellent than any other creature. For whilst every other creature flows from the *common* goodness of the Creator ;[l] this *new* creature flows from his *singular grace* and promise.[m] Whilst every other creature performs the work of *common* providence ;[n] this *new* creature performs the work of *gracious* predestination.[o] Whilst every other rejoices, only in the *natural* benefits of God ; this new creature is loaded with *spiritual* blessings.[p] (5) Instead of an insensible, *stoney* heart, they have a heart of *flesh,* easily affected, which carries the law of God written upon it.[q] (6) From person's dead, they are become spiritually *alive.*[r] (7) They carry about them the Divine Image, which is restored to them, which is their peculiar prerogative, h. e. *original righteousness.*[s] And what is more, (8) They are made partakers of a *divine nature.*[t] Yea, by regeneration, since they are *born of God,*[u] they become the children of God ; not only by adoption, or *declaration,* as Jacob the patriarch adopted Ephraim and Manasseth ;[w] but also by a spiritual *generation.* How are the regenerate *enabled* hereby ![x] How glorious is their *inheritance* ![y] How great is the *liberty* of the sons of God ![b] How free their *access* to God in every difficulty ![c] How great their *security* under the paternal and domestic care of their heavenly Father ![d] (9) They are by this spiritual generation endowed with *eyes,* by which they *can see* the kingdom of God,[e] and *spiritually* discern the spiritual objects of it ;[f] and moreover with a *heart,* by which they are both able and willing *to enter* into the kingdom of God.[g] If now you cast up the sum of all these blessings, good God ! how great doth the *blessedness* of the truly regenerate appear to be ? How careful then should we be to represent it aright ? That such may *congratulate* themselves upon this unspeakable gift of God :[h] That they may be filled with *gratitude* to God :[i] That they may *shew* to others the

greatness

[j] Tit. 2. 14.
[k] 2 Cor. 5. 17.
[l] Psa 104. 31. and 145. 9.
[m] Eph. 2. 4 5.
[n] Acts 17. 25.
[o] Rom. 8. 29. 30. Jam. 1. 18.
[p] Psa 147. 8. &c. 17. 14. 15. Eph. 2. 4. 5. 6. ch. 1. 3.
[q] Ezek. 36. 25. 26.
[r] Eph. 2. 4. 5. 6.
[s] Eph. 4. 23. 24. Col. 3. 10.
[t] 2 Pet. 1. 4.
[u] John 1. 13. & 1 Joh. 5. 14.
[w] Gen. 48. 5.
[x] 1 John 3. 1.
[a] Rom. 8. 15.
[b] Rom 8. 21.
[c] Rom. 8. 15. Gal. 4. 6.
[d] Eph. 2. 18. 19
[e] John 3. 3.
[f] 1 Cor. 2. 14. 15.
[g] John 3. 5.
[h] Ps. 116. 16.
[i] 1 Pet. 1. 3.

k Lu e 8.39.
Mat. 5 16.
1.Pet. 1. 2.

greatnefs of this bleffing, to excite their eager defires and longings after it.[k]

XXXV. *Thirdly.* This fubject reprefents, upon the other hand, the unfpeakable *mifery* of thofe, who are deftitute of the grace of regeneration. Becaufe, (1)

3. It repre-
fents the mi-
fery of the
unregenerate
in fix particu-
lars.

They *cannot* even *fee* the kingdom of God, much lefs enter therein; hence they are utterly excluded from the very threfhold of eternal falvation.[l] (2) So long

l John 3. 3.5.
m John 1. 13.

as they are not born of God,[m] they are born of their

n Joh.8.42.44
o 2Tim.2.26.

father the devil, and fo are the children of the devil,[n] entangled in his fnares.[o] (3) They are fpiritually *dead*

p Eph.2. 1. 5.
Ezek 37.1.2
q 1 Cor.2.14.

in fins,[p] they fee not the things of the fpirit[q]—have hearts of *ftone*—are *obftinate* in wickednefs, and are

r Acts 7. 51.

immoveable to that which is good.[r] They are alfo

s Ezek.36.25.
t Eph.4.18.19
u Jer. 6. 1
x Acts 7. 51.

ftupid, infenfible, impenetrable by any moral operations of the Holy Spirit.[s] [t] Yea, they are *ftriving* againft the fpirit:[u] They are not *fubject* to the law of God, neither

z Róm. 8. 7.
compared
with 2 Cor.
3. 3.

indeed *can* they be.[x] [z] So that you might fooner fqueeze *water* from a *ftone*, than excite repentance in them. They are like ftones, *cold*, deftitute of all warmth, of all *fpiritual* love towards God, his grace,

a Pf. 32. 9.
b Róm. 1.31.

or the falvation of their own fouls:[a] They are with-out natural affection (*aftorgoi*;)[b] and from all thefe things, furely without the *covenant of grace*; for God

c Mat.22. 32.

is not a God of the *dead*.[c] (4) So long as they remain *unregenerate*, it were better for them not to have been *born*, which our Saviour exprefly declares concerning

d Mark14 21.
compared
with Job 3. 3
—9. Jer. 20.
14. 15.
e Eph. 2. 10.

Judas;[d] and the unregenerate, in hell hereafter, will curfe the day of their *birth*. (5) So long as they are not the *workmanfhip* of God by the grace of regenera-tion,[e] it were better for them never to have been *cre-ated* by God, before not to have been made *men*; but rather the loweft and moft defpicable reptiles: becaufe from the immortality of their fouls, immortal, yea,

f Mat. 25.41.
Isa. 66 24.

eternal *mifery* awaits them; whilft thefe reptiles will be forever infenfible. (6) So long as they are not, by regeneration, brought back to God, they are *alienated from*

from the life of God,[g] *are afar off* from God,[h] with an immense *gulph,* as it were, fixed between them.[i] They are cast out with Cain from the *presence of God* ;[k] are *without* God in the world ;[l] are afar off from the *know-ledge* of God, and of divine things;[m] seeking after God, as it were, by *feeling* after him in the dark ;[n] afar off also from the *love* and *saving grace* of God ;[o] and also from *Christ,* from the *commonwealth* of Israel, from the covenants of promise and from all hope of salvation.[p] To paint in the most lively manner this great misery of the unregenerate is of great service; (1) To *our-selves,* that we may hence conceive a greater *horror* of that state, and groan out with David, *Create in me a clean heart, O God, and renew a right spirit within me,*[q] *that we might work out our own salvation with fear and trembling: for it is God which worketh in us, both to will and to do.*[t] And that we might *rejoice with trembling,*[r] in that we have received the grace of regeneration. (2) It may be of service to *others,* who are yet in an un-regenerate state, that, by divine assistance, *they might awake (or recover themselves) from the snares of the devil,* ★ *by which, they are led captive at his will.*[t]

XXXVI. *Fourthly:* This subject admonishes us that we should *avoid* more than we would the most venomous animal, the *resting,* in the business of our souls salvation, in *any* thing, however specious, short of *regeneration.* And that for the following reasons. (1) It appears from the most solemn repeated asserti-ons of our Saviour, that it is impossible, without re-generation, either to *see* or *enter* into, the kingdom of God.[s] (2) Whatever *is born of the flesh,* h i. e. proceeds from a *carnal* unregenerate man, is only *carnal.*[w] (3) Thousands, by taking things *natural* for things *spiri-tual,* nature for *grace,* a good natural disposition for regeneration, have miserably deceived themselves, and under this deception have perished eternally ;[x] and our

★ In our translation "who are taken captive by him at his will."

Side notes:
[g] Eph. 4. 17. 18
[h] Eph. 2. 13. 17
[i] Luke 16. 26.
[k] Gen. 4. 14.
[l] Eph. 2. 12.
[m] Eph. 4. 18.
[d] Cor. 2. 14.
[n] Acts 17. 27.
[o] Isa. 59. 2.
[p] Eph. 2. 12.

For what end this represen-tation is to be made.
[q] Psal. 51. 12.

[r] Phil. 2. 13.
[s] Psal. 2. 11.

[t] 2 Tim. 2. 26.

4. That we should not rest in any thing which is not abso-lutely con-nected with regeneration.

[s] John 3. 3. 5.
[w] John 3. 6.

[x] Luk. 18. 11. 12.

ourSaviour declares that Publicans and Harlots should enter into the kingdom of God *before* the Pharisees.[a] Particularly we should avoid, in the business of our salvation, resting, (1) In a more *virtuous, natural* disposition: By which thro' a certain native *goodness of temper*, as tho' they were formed of pure clay, some among the Heathen have been more inclined than others, to mildness, humanity, civility, clemency, equity, and the like; upon which account the more moral *Pharisee* gives thanks to God, that he was not like other men, particularly the Publican, who was standing near him.[b] Nor, (2) should we rest in any natural *gifts* which may be acquired; wherein one excelleth another among the Gentiles, and likewise among pretended Christians. v. g. In learning, wisdom, prudence, skill in mechanicks or philosophy, v.g. such as Ahithophel,[y] Bezaleel and Aholiab[d] were possessed of. Nor, (3) in *moral virtues*, from which the Gentiles are said to have the *law of God written upon their hearts*,[g] yea they are said to do, *by nature, the things contained in the law*;[z] in which virtues, (v. g.) Plato, Cato, Scipio, Cicero, Aristides, Seneca, and the Antonini, a thousand degrees exceeded Cataline, Caligula, Nero, Heliogabulus, and others. Yea the Gentiles have herein some times out-done God's *professing* people. v. g. Tyre and Sidon excelled the inhabitants of Bethsaida and Chorazin:[g] The Sodomites, the inhabitants of Capernaum;[h] and the queen of the South, the Jews.[i] Nor, (4) may we rest in any *ecclesiastical* or external duties of religion; such as the *acknowledgement* of the truth,[k] the *profession* of it,[l] *disputing for it*,[m] a frequent *attendance* upon holy exercises; the use of the sacraments,[o] bestowing of alms,[p] fasting,[q] suffering martyrdom for the truth,[r] *preaching* the word,[t] or in a *zealous* profession.[u] Nor, (5) may we rest in any kind of external *righteousness*,[a] a conversation that is morally honest,[b] or a blamelessness as to their righteousness of *the law.*

a Mat. 21. 31.

In what things we should by no means rest.

b Luke 18.11. 12.

y 2 Sam.16.23
d Exod.31.2.
e Rom.2 15.
z ver. 14.
g Mat.11.21.
h v 23.
i Mat 12 24
k Rom.2.18.
22. 1 Cor. 13.2.
d Rom 2.17
Mat.8.21.22.
m 1 Chr.1.19. 20. Luke 18. 11 Isa.i.15.
o 1 Cor. 10. 2.3.4 Acts 8. 13 Gal.5.2 6 or.11. 27
p Mat 6.12.
1 Cor. 13-3.
q Luke 18.12.
t 1 Cor.15.3.
u Mat 7.21 22 1 Cor. 13.
x Phil. 3. 6.
a Mat. 5. 20.
b Luke 18.11. 12.

law.[e] Nor, (6) may we reft in the gifts of *common* grace ;[d] fuch as, (1) the common *illumination* of the Holy Spirit ;[e] in confequence of which, we may acknowledge the faving truth, receive it with joy, profefs it courageoufly, and preach it with zeal : (2) The powerful *reſtraining* influences of the fpirit.[f] (3) Some kind of *deteſtation* and avoidance of enormous crimes.[g] (4) A kind of *repentance* for grofs fins, wherein we acknowledge them, are forry for them, confefs them, and in a degree reform our lives, as Judas did :[h] (5) An *external* obfervance of the law and precepts of God [i] In all thefe things therefore, and many others, a man muft never *reſt*, in the great bufinefs of his falvation, if he means not to be deceived ; for all thefe things may be found in perfons deftitute of the fpirit, or his *regenerating* influences, arifing merely from *fleſhly* principles, therefore they may be only of a *carnal* nature :[k] Altho' in the truly regenerate thefe things may take their origin from the fpirit or the fpiritual life infufed. Wherefore it is abfolutely neceffary, that in all thefe things, we accurately diftinguifh the *nature* of them from the grace of regeneration, and mark their defects, from which we may clearly know, that they flow not from the *fpirit,* or the fpiritual life of regeneration ; but from the *fleſh,* that is from unregenerate nature. Thofe *moral* duties therefore differ from fpiritual ones. 1. As to their *origin* ; for whilft fpiritual things originate from the *fpirit,* [l] and are the fruit of the fpirit,[m] and proceed from the law of God, written by the fpirit upon the heart ;[n] thofe moral duties are effected *merely* by induftry, ftudy and practice, and are excited by the powers of free will, and are therefore only the works of *nature,* not of the *fpirit.* 2. They differ as to the *rule* : whilft *fpiritual* duties conform themfelves to the rule of the *new* creature,[o] and they, that are fpiritual walk after the *fpirit,* [p] and according to the will of God ;[q] the *morality* of the unregenerate

[e] Phil. 3. 6.
[d] Heb. 6. 4.
[e] Num. 24. 3 4

[f] Gen. 20. 6.
[g] 1 Cor. 5. 1.

[h] Math. 27. 3,
4. 5.
[i] Kings 21 27.
[i] Mat. 19. 18.
19. 20.

[k] John 3. 6.

How moral duties differ from fpiritual.
[l] John 3 5.
[m] Gal. 5. 22.
[n] Jer. 31. 33.
Ezek. 36. 26.
27.

[o] Gal. 6. 15.
[p] Rom. 8. 1.
[q] Mat. 6. 10.

H

unregenerate is regulated by a kind of *mediocrity*, which reafon and the fentiments of wife men have fixed. Therefore this morality is not obedience performed unto *God*, but to *reafon* and wife men. 3. They differ as to the *end* : whilft the *regenerate*, in the performance of *fpiritual* duties, aim at the *glory* of God, ' and after union and communion with him, in which their greateft happinefs confifteth : ' The *unregenerate* in their *moral* duties feek chiefly their *own* glory and intereft, as was evidently the cafe with the Pharifees : °. or if fomething higher excites them to the purfuit of *virtue*, at moft 'tis only the *beauty* of virtue, as being *agreeable* to reafon. 4., They differ as to the immediate *caufe* : whilft fpiritual duties flow from faith, ' which accounts as fin whatfoever is not of *itfelf*, however fpecious it may appear : " Thefe *moral* duties know nothing of *faith*, they grow from the feeds of *nature*, and are watered by exercife, without any earneft feeking of divine affiftance. 5. They differ as to the *foundation* : whilft all *fpiritual* duties have their exiftence, and are performed in *Chrift*, without whom we *can do nothing*," and by whom we *can do all things* ;* nor are they acceptable to God, except in Chrift the beloved ; * as, by his righteoufnefs he covers, and makes amends for, all the defects of thefe duties, and fo prefents them to his father : The *morality* of the unregenerate hath *nothing* of Chrift in it, and is therefore but the *tares of nature*, their own righteoufnefs, and like a *menftruous* garment, abominable in the fight; of God. * 6. They differ as to the *affection* of humility : whilft *fpiritual* exercifes are joined with a conftant fenfe and acknowledgement of their native unfitnefs and corruption, and confequently with profound humility : ᵇ This *morality puffeth up* and favours rankly of pride and arrogance.

ᶠ1 Cor.1o.31.
Phil. 1. 2o.
ᵃ Pf. 16. 5. &
73. 25.

°᷍ Mat.6.2.5.

ᵗ Rom. 1. 17.
Gal. 2. 2o.
ᵘRom.14.25.

ᵛ John 15.5.
ˣ Phil. 4. 13.
ᶻ Eph. 1.

ᵃ If 64 6.
ᵇ Luke17 10,
and 18. 13
2 Cor. 3. 5
ᶜMat.6.2.5.8.
Luke 18. 11.
1 2 If. 58. 2.3.
Mat. 7. 26.

XXXVII,

XXXVII. *Fifthly.* This subject recommends to us, an impartial *examination* of ourselves, that we may know, whether we are truly regenerate or not. Altho' the *first* act or-principle of spiritual life, which is conferred in regeneration, be not evident *of itself*, any more than the *first* act or principle of natural life, or any habit or virtue : It is however very conspicuous in its *operations*, which it puts forth in conversion : and altho' a person, before one of good *moral conversation*, cannot easily be certain that he is *not* regenerate, because the life of regeneration may sometimes, like seed in the earth, lie hid for a time : however he that is truly regenerated and converted can, from the *fruits* of the spirit, [a] be absolutely certain of his regeneration and conversion : [e] Before he, that brings *not* forth fruits, meet for repentance, may justly *doubt* of his regeneration, so as to be sensible that he stands in need of it. By what evidences then shall I certainly know that I am regenerated ? I answer by these which follow, 1. Whoever experiences within himself a general *renovation*, by which, from a *carnal*, worldly man, he becomes *spiritual* and heavenly, he without doubt is regenerate : for regeneration is the *renovation* of the Holy Spirit,[f] and a regenerate person is a *new creature*,[g] who hath received a *new* heart, a *new* spirit,[h] and is *transformed* into the *image of God*,[i] so that it is no longer *he that liveth*, but *Christ in him*.[k] 2. Whoever, instead of his former *blindness*, experiences new *light*, by which he can know and discover spiritual objects in a *spiritual* manner, he is most certainly regenerate.[l] 3. Whoever, in his heart and will, experiences a new *propensity* towards spiritual objects, he without doubt is a regenerate person.[m] 4. Whoever in the *affections* or passions of his soul, in love and hatred, desire and aversion, joy and sorrow ; likewise anger, fear and courage, experiences a more *spiritual* constitution than before ; he is most certainly regenerate.[n] 5. Whoever seriously strive after *growth* in spiritual things, that they may

increase

Margin references:
° 1 Pet. 2. 2. Matth. 18. 3. ᵖ Eph 2. 10. Col 1 10 Acts 9 6. Rom. 1. 9 & 7. 22. 2 Pet.1.4.5 6. 7. 8.

Just reasons, reasons for doubting of one's regeneration.

q Joh 3.6. ʳ 2 Tim 2.25 26 Eph.2.1.2 3. 4 5. Rom. 8. 13. &6 12.&7 4 5 6. ˢ Joh.8. 45. 2 Tim. 2. 25. 26. ᵗ Mat 5 20 Lu.18 11. ᵘ 2 Ph. 3 4 5.6 Rom. 2. 17.

6. This subject inculcates upon us, to strive earnestly for the regeneration of others.

Motives thereto.

ʷ 7 Tim. 3. 5. Mat.7.21.22. 23.11. 8 2. Ezek 33. 31. 32.1Cor.13.3 ˣ Jer 31. 19. Acts 2. 37. ˣ Acts 26. 17 ᵃ 8.2Cor.5.18 19. 2 Tim. 2. 25. 26. 27. ᵇ 1Cor. 3. 9. 2 Cor. 6 1. ᶜ 1Cor.4. 15. ᵈ Mat.16. 26. Luke 9 25. ᵈProv. 11.30 Mat. 4 19.ᵉ Heb. 2. 10. 13. 1 Thef. 2. 19. 2 Cor. 1. 14. Dan. 12. 3. ʸ Ezek. 3. 18. 20. Jer. 48. 10. 1 Cor. 9. 16. 17.

---

increase more and more in the things which pertain to the kingdom of God, and be changed for the better; they without doubt are regenerate.° 6. Whoever are *inclined* to every good work, are most certainly regenerated; for we are in Christ Jesus, by regeneration, *created unto good works.*ᵖ On the other hand, the following characters have just reason to doubt of their regeneration, (1) As many as *live* not after the *spirit,* but after the *flesh* ; for whatsoever *is born of the flesh, is flesh* ; q who are under the *dominion* of sin, led captive by the snares of satan.ʳ (2) All they, who *despise* and account as of no value the *means* of grace and salvation.ˢ (3) Whoever *rest* in a civilly *honest* and pharisaical life.ᵗ (4) Whoever stop in the external *professions* of piety, and labour not for the *internal* exercises of it.ᵘ (5) As many, as were never *deeply* concerned about their salvation, or the spiritual state of their souls.ʷ

XXXVIII. *Sixthly.* This subject inculcates upon us, to strive earnestly for the regeneration of others : which is especially incumbent on the *ministers* of God's word. For since the unregenerate can do nothing towards regenerating *themselves,* 'tis necessary, every one should strive therefor ; they especially whose business God hath made it *ex officio* (from their office,) And for their encouragement herein, it may be well seriously to consider, (1) That they are *called* hereto by God.ˣ (2) That, herein they act as *fellow labourers,* with God.ᵃ (3) That, on this account, they are called *fathers,* because they beget spiritual children.ᵇ (4) How important a thing the human *soul* is.ᶜ (5) How glorious it is to *win* souls to Christ.ᵈ So that Austin not improperly declared, that the conversion of a soul exceeded any *miracle.* (6) How *glorious* it will be for them hereafter, in the last day, to have begotten many to a spiritual life.ᵉ (7) On the other hand, how *disgraceful,* how horrible it will be, to be found guilty of the neglect of *souls.*ʸ But in what manner shall they

labour

labour for the regeneration of others? Anf. 1. By teaching and inftructing them concerning the nature of regeneration as Chrift did Nicodemus.[f] 2. By inculcating the abfolute *neceffity* of regeneration, without which they can neither *fee*, nor *enter* into the kingdom of God.[g] 3. By laying open the unfpeakable *mifery* of thofe who die without regeneration,[h] as in § xxxv. 4. By powerfully reprefenting the happy *condition* of thofe who are truly regenerate, as in § xxxiv. 5. By pointing out the *means*, (*adminicula*) whereby we may become partakers of regenerating grace; fuch as, v. g. (1.) To avoid with Nicodemus[i] intimacy with the unregenerate,[k] and feek, as he did, the company and inftruction of thofe, who can point out to us the life of regeneration.[a] (2) To conceive the *feed* of regeneration[l] the word of God. (3) To urge the promife of the covenant of grace.[m] (4) To groan out with David, *Create within me a clean heart, O God, and renew a right fpirit within me,* &c.[n] 6. By removing *prejudices*, pretences and impediments, by which the unregenerate are wont to block up their way to regeneration; fuch as v. g. (1) That they fhall thereby be obliged to condemn themfelves, and openly expofe all their paft life with the greateft difgrace to themfelves. To which this anfwer may be given, [1] Whatever fmall difgrace it may be, we muft chearfully fubmit to it, if we would avoid eternal difgrace.[o] [2] The very beft of men never were afhamed to confefs their fins and condemn their wicked lives:[p] and by the confent of all chriftians, this is abfolutely neceffary to falvation.[q] [3] 'Tis even an honor to a man, ingenuoufly to retract whatever he hath done amifs,[r] and recount his paft crimes to the glory of divine grace.[s] Obj. 2. That in this way, they muft begin every thing anew, and pull down all that they have been building up before. Anf. What hath been badly built, fhould be pulled down, left it fall of itfelf; as is plainly the cafe

with

The way in which we fhould ftrive for the regeneration of others.
[f] John 3. 4 5.
[g] John 3. 3. 5.
[h] Rom 7. 24.
2 Tim. 2. 26.
Luke 13. 3.

[i] John 3 2.
[k] Acts 2. 38. 40

[a] 1 Cor. 4 15. Prov. 13. 20. Eph. 4. 29.
[l] 1 Pet. 1. 23.
1 Cor. 4. 15.
[m] Ezek. 36 25. 26 27. and 11. 19. Jer. 32. 39.
[n] Pf. 51. 12.

[o] Dan. 12. 2.

[p] Pf. 51.——
[q] 1 Cor. 11. 31.
Prov. 28. 13.
[r] 2 Cor. 3. 2.
[s] 1 Tim. 1 13. Tit. 3. 3. 4.
1 Cor. 6. 10. 11

with buildings, whose foundations are rotten and poor.' Obj. 3. That by bringing into doubt all their former conduct, they shall be brought into a state of despair. Anf. (1) It is better to despair here, where there is *hope*, than hereafter to be in *hopeless* despair forever. (2) This salutary despair of their past wrong ways, is really a substantial *hope*, yea, an undoubted means of bringing them back into the way of eternal salvation. Obj. 4. That they can't come up to that *strictness of life*, which belongs to regeneration and the new creature. Anf. (1) 'Tis 'thro' *straits* and difficulties that we arrive to any thing glorious. " (2) The way is not difficult; but pleasant, to the truly regenerate." Obj. 5. That hereby they shall become exposed, to the censures, reproach and persecutions of the world. Anf. [1] This is the common lot of Christians; and happy is he, in the opinion of Christ, who is *not offended* hereby. ˣ [2] In these very *afflictions* consisteth one of the christian *beatitudes.* ª 7. We should seek the regeneration of sinners, by praying for them, that God would give *success* to his own institutions, ᵇ that he would quicken, illuminate, and renew the unregenerate, and deliver, from their hearts of stone, those who need regeneration, &c.ᶜ Nor need any suspect that in all this, they talk only to the deaf, or knock at the doors of the dead ; since, (1) By doing what belongs to them, leaving the success to God, they perform their *bounden* duty and will deliver their own souls. ᵈ (2) Altho' it may so happen that they are treating with those, who are *spiritually* dead ; yet they are treating with those who are *naturally* alive, who are endowed with understanding and will, and can understand things in their grammatical and historical sense. (3) Because God, in the use of such means, is wont to bestow the grace of regeneration. ᵍ

XXXIX.

Margin references:

ᵗ Mat. 7. 26.

ᵘMat. 7. 13 14

ʷ Mat. 11 28. 29. Rom. 7. 22.

ˣ Mat. 11. 6
1 Pet. 4. 12.
1 Thef. 3. 3.
ªMat. 5. 10. 11
1 Pet. 4. 14.
ᵇ 1 Cor. 3. 5.
6 7. /
ᶜ Eph. 1. 16.
17. 18. Rom.
15. 13.

ᵈ Ezek 3. 17.
—21.

ᵍ If. 59. 21.
Rom. 15 18.
19. 1 Cor. 3 5
6. 7.

·· XXXIX. *Seventhly.* This subject may serve to exort the *regenerate,* diligently to apply to the duties meet for regeneration; viz. (1.) That they acknowledge the unspeakable *grace* of God, bestowed on them in regeneration, by his mere *good pleasure,* while so many thousands are passed by; and that they rejoice therein.[a] (2.) That sensible of this unspeakable benefit, they are abundant in ingenuous *thankfgiving* to God.[b] (3.) That they wholly *depend* on God, as the original fountain of their spiritual life;[c] who worketh in us, both to will, and to do.[d] (4.) That in the use of appointed means, they strive for a continual *increase* of the spiritual life, communicated to them by regeneration.[e] (5.) For this end, they should be importunate with God, in fervent prayer.[f] (6.) Especially should they endeavour with all engagedness to bring forth into the *second* acts (or exercises) the *first act* of spiritual life which they received by regeneration; as they, who *live* by the spirit, should also *walk* in the spirit;[g] and therefore, (7.) Being drawn, they should *run;*[h] being delivered from the heart of stone, they should *make to themselves a new heart, and a new spirit;*[i] being circumcised, *they should circumcise themselves to the Lord, and take away more and more the foreskin of their heart.*[k] h. e. Being now made alive by regeneration, they should put off, by *conversion* and repentance, concerning their *former conversation, the old man, and be renewed in the spirit of their mind; and that they might put on the new man which after God is created in righteousness and true holiness.*[l] And that they bear in mind that they are, by regeneration, the *workmanship* of God, created in *Christ Jesus unto good works, that they might walk in them.*[m] But these things belong to *conversion and sanctification,* which are the end of regeneration, as the *second* acts (or exercises) are the end of the *first* act or principle.

Marginal notes:

7 This subject recommends to the regenerate, that they apply diligently to the duties meet for regeneration. What they are.

[a] James 1.17. 18. Eph. 2.5. 6. compared with Luke 15. 32.
[b] 1 Pet. 1.3.4.
[c] 2 Cor. 4. 4.
[d] 6.
[e] Phil. 2 13.
[f] 1 Pet. 2 2.
[g] Pf 51. 12.
[h] Gal. 5. 25. Rom. 8. 1.
[i] Cant. 1. 4.
[j] Ezek. 18 31.
[k] Jer. 4. 4.
[l] Eph. 4. 22. 23. 24.
[m] Eph. 2. 10.

APPENDIX.

FROM the Westminster confession of faith, chap. 10. of effectual calling. "All those whom God hath predestinated unto life, and those only, he is pleased in his appointed and accepted time, effectually to call by his word and Spirit, out of that state of sin and death, in which they are by nature, to grace and salvation by Jesus Christ ; enlightening their minds, spiritually and savingly to understand the things of God ; taking away their heart of stone, and giving unto them an heart of flesh ; renewing their wills, and by his *almighty power determining them* to that which is good ; and effectually drawing them to Jesus Christ ; yet so as they come most freely, being made willing by his grace.

II. This effectual call is of God's free and special grace alone, not from any thing at all foreseen in man, who is altogether *passive* therein, until being quickened and renewed by the Holy Spirit, he is thereby enabled to answer this call, and to embrace the grace offered and conveyed in it."

Dr. Twiss Prolocutor of the assembly of divines at Westminster in his Vindiciæ Gratiæ, &c. page 15. of the preface, thus defines efficacious grace. "We explain efficacious grace to be an Operation of God affecting the will of man, which is not moral but *physical*, that is immediately and really working in us to do whatsoever good we perform, determining the will to action, but yet so as that it acts freely."

Part III. Page 124. "We do not deny that God acts by (moral) suasion ; but he acts also by a *physical* operation, which immediately and immutably affects the

the will and that by an irrefiftible agency : For as to moral fuafien, it is plain the agent acts only in the way of placing objects before the mind, which neither acts upon the will immediately, nor at all after the manner of an efficient caufe, but merely after the manner of a final caufe. This divine concurrence is of that kind that neither men nor angels can refift. We fay this action of God cannot be refifted; for this reafon, that it doth not confift in moral fuafion, fo as to be in its nature refiftible ; but in an immediate change of the will, which cannot properly be called either refiftible or irrefiftible with refpect to the will upon which it acts : For that, properly fpeaking, is irrefiftible, which a perfon *can not* refift tho' he *wills* to. But fuppofing a man fhould will otherwife, than God worketh in him to will; he not only *could* refift, but herein actually *would* refift : But upon this fuppofition it would follow, that God did not work in him by changing his will ; for if he changed his will, hereby of unwilling he would make him willing. But if we fuppofe a man to will any thing from the operation of God, it cannot be that he fhould not will it or will the contrary. For God himfelf cannot make a thing to be and not to be at the fame time."

Dr. Ridgley, in his expofition of the larger catechifm under the anfwer, which treats of effectual calling, Vol. 2. P. 20. gives his fentiments upon the doctrine of regeneration in the following words.

" The firft ftep that he (i. e. God) is pleafed to take in this work, (i. e. the work of effectual calling) is in his implanting a principle of fpiritual life and grace, which is abfolutely neceffary for our attaining to, or receiving advantage by the external call of the gofpel ; this is generally ftlled regeneration, or the new birth ; or, as in the fcripture but now referred to, (viz. Ezek. 36. 26.) *a new heart.* If it be enquired, What we are to underftand by this principle ? We anfwer, That fince principles are only known by thofe effects they produce,

fprings

springs of acting, by the actions themselves, we must be content with this description ; that it is something wrought in the heart of man, whereby he is habitually and prevailingly biassed and inclined to what is good : So that by virtue hereof, he freely, readily, and willingly chooses those things which tend to the glory of God ; and refuses, abhors and flees from what is contrary thereunto ; and, as this more immediately affects the understanding, whereby it is enabled to discern the things which God reveals in the gospel in a spiritual way, it is stiled, his *shining in the heart, to give us the light of the knowledge of his glory, or his giving an eye to see, and an ear to hear.* As it respects the will, it contains in it a power, whereby it is disposed, and enabled to yield the obedience of faith, to what ever God is pleased to reveal to us as a rule of duty, so that we are made willing in the day of his power ; and as it respects the affections, they are all disposed to run i, a right channel, to desire, delight and rejoice in every thing that is pleasing to God, and flee from every thing that is provoking to him. This is that whereby a dead sinner is made alive, and so enabled to put forth living actions.

Concerning this principle of grace, let it be observed, that it is infused, and, not acquired. The first principle or spring of good actions, may, with equal reason, be supposed to be infused into us as Christians, as it is undoubtedly true, that the principle of reasoning is infused into us as men : None ever supposed that the natural power of reasoning may be acquired, tho' a greater facility or degree thereof is gradually attained ; so that power, whereby we are enabled to put forth supernatural acts of grace, which we call a principle of grace, must be supposed to be implanted in us ; which, were it acquired, we could not, properly speaking, be said to be born of God.

From hence I am obliged to infer, that the regenerating act, or implanting this principle of grace, which is,

at

at leaft, in order of nature, antecedent to any act of grace, put forth by us, is the immediate effect of the power of God, which none, who fpeak of regeneration as a divine work, pretend to deny ; and therefore I cannot but conclude, that it is wrought in us *without the inftrumentality of the word, or any of the ordinary means of grace* : My reafon for it is this ; becaufe it is neceffary (from the nature of the thing) to our receiving, improving or reaping any faving advantage by the word, that the fpirit fhould produce the principle of faith ; and to fay, that this is done by the word, is, in effect, to affert that the word produces the principle, and the principle gives efficacy to the word ; which feems to me little lefs than arguing in a circle. The word cannot profit unlefs it be mixed with faith ; and faith cannot be put forth, unlefs it proceeds from a principle of grace implanted ; therefore this principle of grace is not produced by it : We may as well fuppofe, that the prefenting a beautiful picture before a man that is blind, can enable him to fee ; or the violent motion of a withered hand, produce ftrength for action, as we can fuppofe that the prefenting the word, in an objective way, is the inftrument whereby God produces that internal principle, by which we are enabled to embrace it. Neither would this fo well agree with the *idea* of its being a new creature, or our being *created unto good works* ; for then it ought rather to be faid, we are created by faith, which is a good work : This is, in effect, to fay that the principle of grace is produced by the inftrumentality of that which fuppofes its being implanted, and is the refult and confequence thereof.

I am forry that I am obliged in this affertion, to appear, at leaft, to oppofe what has been maintained by many divines of great worth ; who have in all other refpects, explained the doctrine of regeneration, agreeably to the mind and will of God, and the analogy of faith. It may be the principal difference between this explication,

explication, and their's is, that they speak of regeneration in a large sense, as including in it, not barely the implanting the principle, but the exciting it, and do not sufficiently distinguish between the principle as implanted and deduced into act ; for, I readily own, that the latter is, by the instrumentality of the word, though I cannot think the former so ; or, it may be, they consider the principle as excited ; whereas I consider it as created, or wrought in us ; and therefore can no more conclude that the new creation is wrought by an instrument, than I can, that the first creation of all things was.

And I am ready to conjecture, that that which leads many divines into this way of thinking, is the sense in which they understand the words of the apostle : Being *born again, not of corruptible seed, but of incorruptible, by the word of God which liveth and abideth forever :* And elsewhere, *Of his own will, begat he us with the word of truth, that we should be a kind of first-fruits of his creatures.* Whereas this doth not so much respect the implanting the principle of grace, as it does our being enabled to act from that principle ; and 'tis as tho' he should say, he hath made us believers, or induced us to love and obey him by the word of truth, which supposes a principle of grace to have been implanted ; otherwise the w rd of truth would never have produced these effects. Regeneration may be taken, not only for our being made alive to God, or created unto good works, but for our putting forth living actions, proceeding from that principle which is implanted in the soul. I am far from denying, that faith, and all other graces are wrought in us by the instrumentality of the word ; and it is in this sense that some, who treat on this subject, explain their sentiments, when they speak of being born again by the word : Therefore I persuade myself, that I differ from them only in the acceptation of words, and not in the main substance of the doctrine they maintain."

Doct. Ridgley quotes Charnock, with approbation, concerning

concerning the diftinction between regeneration and converfion, in the following words. "Regeneration is a
fpiritual change ; converfion is a fpiritual motion ; in
regeneration there is a power conferred ; converfion is
the exercife of this power ; in regeneration there is given
us a principle to turn ; converfion is our actual turning ;
in the covenant, the new heart, and God's putting the
fpirit into them, is diftinguifhed from their walking in
his ftatutes, from the firft ftep we take in the way of
God, and is fet down as the caufe of our motion : In
renewing us God gives us a power ; in converting us
he excites that power. Men are naturally dead, and
have a ftone upon them ; regeneration is a rolling away
the ftone from the heart, and a raifing to newnefs of life ;
and then converfion is as natural to a regenerate man,
as motion is to a living body : A principle of activity
will produce action. The firft reviving us is wholly
the act of God, without any concurrence of the creature ;
but, after we are revived, we do actively and volunta-
rily, live in his fight. Regeneration is the motion of
God in the creature ; converfion is the motion of the
creature to God, by virtue of that firft principle ; from
this principle all the acts of believing, repenting, mor-
tifying, quickening do fpring. In all thefe a man is active ; in the other he is merely paffive."*

Thus far Mr. Charnock.

Doct. Ridgley further obferves, (vol. 2. p. 23) relative to our paffivity in regeneration. "I cannot but
take notice of a queftion which frequently occurs under
this head, viz. Whether man in the firft moment thereof, viz. in regeneration, be merely paffive, tho' active
in every thing that follows after it ? This we cannot
but affirm, not only againft the *Pelagians*, but others,
whofe method of treating the doctrine of divine grace,
feems to agree with theirs. This is fufficiently evident,
not only from the impotency of corrupt nature, as to
what is good, but it's utter averfenefs thereto, and from
the

---

* See Charnock on regeneration, Vol. 2. page 70, 71.

the work's being truly and properly divine; or (as has been before obferved) the effect of almighty power. *This is not a controverfy of late date*; but has been either defended or oppofed, ever fince *Auguftine*'s and *Pelagius*'s time."

With respect to preparatory works, Doct. Ridgly, feems well to agree with Van Maftricht. Upon this point he quots Mr. Charnock, in the following words. "Man cannot prepare himfelf for the new birth: He hath indeed a fubjective capacity for grace, above any other creature in the inferior world; and this is a kind of natural preparation, which other creatures have not; a capacity, in regard of the powers of the foul, tho' not in refpect of the prefent difpofition of them. He hath an underftanding to know, and when it is enlightened to know God's law; a will to move and run, and when enlarged by grace, to run in the ways of God's commandments; fo that he ftands in an immediate capacity to receive the life of grace, upon the breath and touch of God, which a ftone doth not; for in this it is neceffary, that rational faculties fhould be put as a foundation of fpiritual motions. Tho' the foul be thus capable, as a fubject, to receive the grace of God, yet it is not therefore capable as an agent, to prepare itfelf for it; or produce it. It is capable to receive the truths of God; but as the heart is ftony, it is incapable to receive the impreffions of thofe truths. Charnock on regeneration. Vol. 2. p. 147, 148.

Mr. Willard, one of the moft noted New-England divines, in his Expofition upon the leffer catechifm, under the anfwer which refpects effectual calling, p. 433, 434, thus obferves,

"1. There is fomething habitually wrought in the man, whereby he is capacitated and difpofed to believe in Chrift. And this is ufually called *paffive converfion*. 2. There is fomething done *actually*, by the man in the exciting of this power fo created in him, in which he applies

applies thofe graces or powers in him, to their objects, and exercifeth them ; and particularly his faith, in clof-ing with, and embracing of Jefus Chrift exhibited in the promife ; and is in the gofpel called believing.—Again, he fays, The *act* of faith doth neceffarily fuppofe the *habit* of it, or the power of believing. All acts require a power fuitable and fufficient for them ; nor can any a-gent go beyond its ability : No effect can exceed the vertue of its caufe : fo that a man muft have faith, in order to his exerting it.

Again. There is no *co-operation* of the man with the fpirit in the producing of the habit of faith in him. He is a fubject but not an agent. He contributes nothing at all to it, but it is wholly put into him by another hand. It is a *creating work*, and that belongs to God alone. Eph. 2. 10. It is a refurrection, and that belongs entirely to the divine Omnipotency. Eph. 1. 19. It is a *regeneration*, and none ever helped to beget himfelf, yea, being a *fpiritual regeneration*, none but the fpirit can effect it.

The means themfelves have no efficacy in the production of this habit by moral fuafion. Not but that the fpirit ufeth the means in order to his bringing about this work in us. *Ezekiel* was to prophefy in order to the dry bones living. Ezek. 37. 9, 10. The means are properly accommoda-ted to work on man as a moral agent, rationally, by evi-dence or demonftration, by convictions, awakenings, encouragements, and the fpirit comes with them as he fees meet, and gives them fuch an operation : But either their operation is common, and that can at moft be but preparatory ; or it is faving, and then it fuppofeth this habit in them. Moral fuafion can do only on a fubject capable. Come to the grave of a dead man, and make never fo grave an oration to him, tell him what a mife-rable condition a ftate of death is, and what benefits ac-company the living, and fo beg of him to rife and live ; And what will this do ? There muft be faith, to receive Chrift, e'er the endeavours to perfuade men produce

the

the act of believing on him, *and this is an operation more than merely ethical or moral."*

Page 435. " All the orthodox consent, that there must be a *new power* put into the man in order to his believing in Christ. That a man can no more of himself come up to the terms of the new covenant, than keep the law of the first covenant. They that deny this are unacquainted with the efficacy of the apostacy, or energy of *original sin* in man. Philosophy tells us that live actions require life in the agent. And spiritual actions must derive from a spiritual life; gracious actions must flow from grace. Call this an habit or a virtue, or a principle; it must be an ability to do these things, which it had not naturally, but must be given it.

This power or ability can be produced by no other, but the Spirit of God. And that because it requires Omnipotency, to the producing of it; and there is none almighty but he. None but he that could make a world, bring light out of darkness, raise the dead, can do this. ——Indeed the Spirit of God in these works find only Impotency in the subject but no resistence; whereas here he meets with, not only a total debility in the creature to join with him in it, but also a malignant opposition to it; there being nothing which the heart of man is more averse to, than coming to Christ and believing in him."

Page 442. As to the necessity of (a legal) conviction or preparation, he thus observes. " This conviction hath no causal influence unto passive conversion. All the necessity that can be urged on that account, is only that of *concomitancy*. The Spirit of God hath done this in much as were not capable of conviction under and by the means. Judicious divines judge that *Jeremiah* and *John* the *Baptist* were converted before they were born. And it is to be believed that elect infants dying in their infancy, have the new creature formed in them. without which they could not be saved. John 3. 3. *Verily, verily I say unto*

unto thee, except a man be born again, he cannot see the king-dom of God. And poffibly this work is done for others that live, before we are aware of it, who have given evidence of their ferioufnefs from their infancy. However, the man can no more convert himfelf upon thefe convictions, than he could before, nor is it eafier for the fpirit to do it now. Whenever it is done, it muft be a creating power, in which God ufeth *no inftrument, but acts immediately."*

Page 455. There muft be a *renewing change* wrought in the *will,* in order to its being enabled to clofe with Chrift. Could we fuppofe never fo much light let into the underftanding, caufing it to difcern all the precioufnefs of Chrift as he is revealed in the gofpel; yet if the will remain in the fame pofture it is, in the man's natural eftate, it would be impoffible for it to chufe Chrift, and to love him. There muft therefore be a renovation on it. When therefore the apoftle had fpoken of our being *renewed in the image of our mind,* Eph. 4. 23. he exemplifies it with refpect to the will, verf. 24. *And that ye put on the new man, which after God is created in righteoufnefs, and true holinefs.* A new underftanding, without a new heart, will never amount to a thorough converfion. As long as the will remains poffeffed of corrupt lufts, and hath no power in it, it can never embrace Chrift.

This renewing change is wrought, by *creating* a new principle of faving grace in the *will* and *affections.* It is certain that if ever the man believe, he muft have power to believe. This power is that which we call the habit of faith; which habit is not infufed by itfelf, but together with all the other regenerating graces, which are wrought in the foul by the Spirit. This is that which is called the giving of a new heart, and the putting in of a new fpirit, &c. Ezek. 36. 26. Which cannot intend new faculties, but a new faving impreffion of grace on the faculties of the foul in the man.

K   Mr.

Mr. Flavel afferts the *priority* of the work of regeneration to faith in Chrift, in the following words.

"For look as the blood of Chrift is the fountain of all merit, fo the Spirit of Chrift is the fountain of all fpiritual life. And until he quicken us, (i. e.) infufe the principle of divine life into our fouls, we can put forth no hand, or vital act of faith, to lay hold upon Jefus Chrift.—This his quickening work, is therefore the *firft* in order of nature to our union with Chrift; and *fundamental* to all other acts of grace done and performed by us, from our firft clofing with Chrift, throughout the whole courfe of our obedience." *Method of grace, fer. 5.*

Mr. Flavel's firft head in the fame difcourfe is, "Briefly to reprefent the neceffary *antecedency* of this quickening work of the Spirit, to our *firft* clofing with Chrift by faith. This, (he fays) will eafily let itfelf into your underftanding, if you will but confider the nature of the vital act of faith ; which is the foul's receiving of Chrift, and refting upon him for pardon and falvation."

After having infifted upon this *antecedency* of regeneration to faith, he ftarts this *queftion*, and gives the following *folution.*

"*Queft.* But here it may be doubted, and objected againft this pofition. If we cannot believe till we are quickened with fpiritual life, as you fay, and cannot be juftified till we believe, as all fay, then it will follow, that a regenerate foul may be in ftate of condemnation for a time and confequently perifh, if death fhould befall him in that juncture."

"*Sol.* To this I return ; That when we fpeak of the *priority* of this quickening work of the Spirit to our actual believing, we rather underftand it of the priority of *nature*, than of *time*, the nature and order of the work requiring it to be fo ; a vital principle muft, in order of nature be infufed, *before* a vital act can be exerted. Firft make the tree good, and then the fruit good : And admit we fhould grant fome priority in *time* alfo to this

quickening

quickening principle, before actual faith ; yet the abſur-
dity mentioned would be no way conſequent upon this
conceſſion : For as the vital act of faith quickly follows
the regenerating principle, ſo the ſoul is abundantly ſe-
cured againſt the danger objected ; God never beginning
any ſpecial work of grace upon the ſoul, and then leaving
it, and the ſoul with it, in hazard ; but preſerves both
to the finiſhing and compleating of his gracious deſign,
Phil. 1. 6." *Ibid.*

The ſame author abundantly aſſerts, that regeneration
is a *ſupernatural* effect, produced by the exertion of *almighty power*, and that we are therein *wholly paſſive*. His
very doctrine in the above mentioned diſcourſe is this ;
" That thoſe ſouls, which have union with Chriſt, are
quickened with a *ſupernatural* principle of life by the
Spirit of God *in order thereunto.*"

Again, " As it is ſaid of the two witneſſes, Rev. xi,
11. Who lay dead in a civil ſenſe, three days and an
half, that the ſpirit of life from God entered into them ;
ſo it is here in a ſpiritual ſenſe, the ſpirit of life from
God enters into the dead, carnal heart : it is all by way
of *ſupernatural infuſion.*"——*Ibid.*

Again. "In the next place, according to the method
propoſed, I am obliged to ſhew you, that this quickening work is *wholly ſupernatural* ; it is the *ſole* and *proper*
work of the ſpirit of God. So Chriſt himſelf expreſsly
aſſerts it, in Joh. 3. 6, 8. *That which is born of the fleſh
is fleſh, and that which is born of the ſpirit, is ſpirit :* the
wind bloweth where it liſteth, and thou heareſt the
ſound thereof, but canſt not tell whence it cometh, nor
whither it goeth; ſo is every one that is born of the ſpirit. Believers are the birth, or offspring of the ſpirit,
who produceth the new creature in them in an unintelligible manner even to themſelves. So far is it *above
their own ability to produce*, that it is above their capacity
to underſtand the way of its production.—We can *contribute nothing*, I mean *actively*, to the production of this
principle

principle of life. We may indeed be said to concur *passively*, with the spirit in it ; that is, there is found in us a capacity, aptness or *receptiveness* of this principle of life. Our nature is endowed with such faculties and powers as are meet subjects to receive, and instruments to act this spiritual life : God only quickens the rational nature with spiritual life."

"It is true also, that in the *progress* of sanctification, a man doth actively concur with the spirit ; but in the *production* of this principle he *can do nothing* ; he can indeed perform those external duties that have a remote tendency to it, but he cannot by the power of nature perform any saving act, or contribute any thing more than a *passive* capacity to the implantation of a new principle ; as will appear by the following arguments."

"Arg. 1. He that *actively* concurs to his own regeneration, makes himself to differ ; but this is denied to all regenerate men, 1 Cor. iv. 7. *Who maketh thee to differ from another ? And what hast thou, that thou didst not receive ?*"

"Arg. 2. That to which the scripture ascribes both impotency and enmity with respect to grace, cannot actively, and of itself concur to the production of it : but the scripture ascribes both impotency and enmity to nature, with respect to grace. It denies to it a power to *do any thing* of itself, John xv. 5. And which is less, it denies to it a power to speak a good *word*, Mat. xii. 34. And which is least of all, it denies it power to *think a good thought.* 2 Cor. iii. 5. This impotency, if there were no more, cuts off all pretence of our *active* concurrence. But then, if we consider that it ascribes enmity to our natures, as well as impotency, how clear is the case ! See Rom. viii. 7. *The carnal mind is* ENMITY *against God.* And Col. i. 21. *And you that were* ENEMIES *in your minds by wicked works.* So then nature is so far productive of this principle, as impotency and enmity can enable it to be so."

" Arg.

" Arg. 3. That which is of natural production muſt needs be ſubject to natural diſſolution. That which is born of the fleſh, is fleſh ; a periſhing thing ; for every thing is as its principle is, and there can be no more in the effect than there is in the cauſe. But this principle of ſpiritual life is not ſubject to diſſolution. It is the water which ſprings up into everlaſting life, John iv. 14. The ſeed of God which remaineth in the regenerate, 1 John iii. 9. And all becauſe it is born not of corruptible, but incorruptible ſeed, 1 Pet. 1. 23."

" Arg. 4. If our new birth be our reſurrection, a new creation, yea a victory of our nature, then we cannot *actively* contribute to its production. But under all theſe notions it is repreſented to us in the ſcriptures. It is our reſurrection from the dead, Eph. v. 14. And you know the body is *wholly paſſive* in its reſurrection. But tho' it concurs not, yet it gives pre-exiſtent matter. Therefore the metaphor is deſignedly varied, Eph. iv. 24. Where it is called a *creation* ; in which there is neither active concurrence nor pre-exiſtent matter. But tho' creation excludes pre-exiſtent matter, yet in producing ſomething out of nothing, there is no reluctancy or oppoſition. Therefore to ſhow how purely *ſupernatural* this principle of life is, it is cloathed and repreſented to us in the notion of a *victory*, 2 Cor. x. 23. And ſo leaves all to grace."

" Arg. 5. If nature could *produce*, or *actively concur* to the production of this *ſupernatural* life, then the beſt natures would be ſooneſt quickened with it ; and the worſt natures not at all, or at laſt, and leaſt of all. But contrarily, we find the worſt natures often regenerated, and the beſt left in the ſtate of ſpiritual death. With how many ſweet *homiletical* virtues was the young man adorned ? Mark x. 21. yet graceleſs ; and what a ſink of ſin was *Mary Magdalen*, Luke vii. 37. Yet ſanctified. Thus beautiful Rachel is barren, while Leah bears children. And there is ſcarce any thing that affects and melts

melts the hearts of Chriſtians more, than this comparative conſideration doth, when they conſider veſſels of gold caſt away, and leaden ones choſen for ſuch noble uſes. So that it is plain enough to all wiſe and humble ſouls, that this new life is *wholly of ſupernatural production.*"—*Ibid.*

Again. "But though we cannot pry into theſe ſecrets by the eye of reaſon, yet God hath revealed this to us' in his ¹word, that it is wrought by *his own almighty power,* Eph. i. 19. The apoſtle aſcribes this work to the *exceeding greatneſs of the power of God.* And this muſt needs be, if we conſider, how the ſpirit of God expreſſes it in ſcripture by a new creation ; (i. e.) a giving being to ſomething, out of nothing, Eph. 2. 10. In this it differs from all the effects of human power ; for men always work upon ſome pre-exiſtent matter, but here there is no ſuch matter. All that is in man, the ſubject of this work, is only a *paſſive* capacity, or *receptivity,* but nothing is found in him to *contribute* towards this work. This *ſupernatural* life is not, nor can be educed out of natural principles. This *wholly tranſcends the ſphere of all natural power.*"—*Ibid.*

The teſtimony of this author is alſo very expreſs, that regeneration is effected *inſtantaneouſly.* His words are theſe, "This infuſion of ſpiritual life is done *inſtantaneouſly,* as all *creation*-work is. Hence it is reſembled to that *plaſtic power,* which in a moment made the light to ſhine out of darkneſs ; juſt ſo God ſhines into our hearts,' 2 Cor. iv. 6."

"It is true, a ſoul may be a long time under the preparatory work of the ſpirit ; he may be under convictions and humiliations, purpoſes and reſolutions a long time,—attending the means and ordinances ; but when the ſpirit comes to quicken the ſoul, it is done *in a moment :* even as it is in the infuſion of the rational ſoul, the body is long e're it is prepared and moulded, but when once prepared and ready, it is quickened with the ſpirit of life in an INSTANT." *Ibid.* Doct.

Doct. Wits or Witfius, a noted Dutch divine of the laft age, fometime colleague with *Van Maftricht* in the Profefforfhip at Utrecht; afterwards Regent of the Divinity College of the Sates of Holland and Weft-Friefland, in his *Œconomy of the Covenants* under the head of Effectual Calling, Page 471 of Dr. Crookfhank's tranflation, thus obferves,

"The *external* call will bring none to communion with Chrift, unlefs it be accompanied with the *internal*, which is accomplifhed not only by perfuafion and command, but by the powerful operation of the Spirit. There is a certain call of God, whereby he makes the things, he calls, to exift, by that very call. By fuch a call, *he calleth thofe things which be not, as though they were.* Rom. 4. 17. For, when he faid, let there be light, immediately there was light, Gen. 1. 3. Not unlike this is that internal call of the fpirit, of which the apoftle writes, 2 Cor. 4. 6. *God who commanded the light to fhine out of darknefs, hath fhined in our hearts.*

Here God exerts his infinite power, by which he converts the foul no lefs powerfully than fweetly. He writes his law on their heart, Jer. 31. 33. Puts the reverence of himfelf there, Ezek. 11. 20. And not only calls them from darknefs to his marvellous light; but alfo, by the call, *draws* them, not to ftand ftill in the path of doubtful deliberation, but to *run after him*, Cant. 1. 4. Not only puts them in an equal poife, but turns them. Jer. 31. 18. Not only advifes, but perfuades, and *he is ftronger and prevails*, Jer. 20. 7. Nor does he follicit, but *tranflate*, Col. 1. 13. Not by an ordinary, but by that mighty power, by which he raifed Chrift from the dead. Eph. 1. 20."

Under the head of regeneration, p. 476. he gives this definition of it, "REGENERATION *is that fupernatural act of God, whereby a new and divine life is infufed into the elect perfon, fpiritually dead, and that from the incorruptible feed of the word of God, made fruitful by the infinite power of the*
Spirit.

Spirit. * He then obferves upon the fpiritual death of finners, " that they are fpiritually infenfible of all fpiritual things, and deftitute of all true feeling ;—nor have they any relifh for divine grace, becaufe it has not yet been conferred upon them ; nor any longing after heavenly things, being ignorant of their worth, They are wholly incapable of every act of true life.—The underftanding is overfpread with difmal darknefs. The will has no tendency to things unknown : and thus all the things of God are defpifed by it as mean." Page 478.

"By regeneration a new life is put into the elect, refulting from a gracious union with God and his Spirit. For, what the foul is to the body, that God is to the foul. Moreover, this fpiritual life may be confidered, either by way of *faculty,* and in the *firft act,* in the ufual language of the fchools ; or by way of *operation,* and in the *fecond act.* In the former refpect, it is that *inward constitution* of the foul, whereby it is fitted to exert thofe actions, which are acceptable to God in Chrift, by the power of the fpirit uniting it to God : whether fuch actions immediately flow from that principle, or whether they lie concealed for fome time, as fruits in their feed. In the latter refpect, it is that activity of the living foul, by which it acts agreeably to the command of God, and the example of Chrift.

If we confider this firft principle of life, there is not the leaft doubt, but regeneration is accomplifhed in a moment. For there is no delay in the tranfition from death to life. No intermediate ftate between the regenerate and unregenerate can be imagined fo much as in thought, if we mean regeneration in the firft act : for

one

* Doct. *Witfius* probably intends the fame kind of inftrumentality of the word as Doct. *Van-Maftricht,* when he calls it "*only a moral inftrument* of regeneration," and that not fo properly to regeneration in the firft act, (which feems to confift, according to thefe authors, in fructifying or making fruitful the word, or rather in laying a foundation for the words becoming fruitful, in which the word cannot be an inftrument) as to regeneration in the fecond act or confequent exercifes ; fee extracts from Doct. Ridgley.

one is either dead or alive : either the child of God, or of the devil ; either in the way to salvation or damnation. There neither is, nor can be any medium here.

Hence it appears, there are no preparations antecedent to the first beginning of regeneration ; because previous to that, nothing but mere death in the highest degree is to be found in the person to be regenerated. *When we were DEAD IN SINS,* he hath quickened us together with Christ, Eph. 2. 5. And indeed the scripture represents man's conversion by such similitudes, as show, that all preparations are entirely excluded ; sometimes calling it a *new regeneration* to which, certainly, none can contribute any thing of himself : But yet, as natural generation presupposes some dispositions in the matter ; so, that we may not imagine any such thing to be in ourselves but from God, we have this held forth by the similitude of a *resurrection* ; in which a body is restored from matter, prepared by no qualifications : yet because here, certainly is matter, but in the resurrection of the soul there is nothing at all, therefore we have added the figure of a *creation*, Ps. 51· 10. Eph. 2. 10. By which we are taught, that a new creature exists from a spiritual nothing, which is sin ; but as there was not something in nothing, to assist and sustain creation ; so there was nothing to oppose and resist ; but sin is so far from submitting to what God does, that it is reluctant thereto, and in an hostile manner at enmity with him : accordingly the other images did not fully complete the idea of this admirable action, till at length it is called the *victory* of God : Victory, I say, over the devil who maintains his palace, Luke 11. 21, and effectually worketh in the children of disobedience, Eph. 2. 2. All these operations of God tend to exclude, as much as possible, all preparations from the beginning of our regeneration."

He then goes on to censure the *Semi-pelagians* of Merseilles, " who insisted that a man comes to the grace whereby we are regenerated in Christ, by a natural faculty ;

L   culty ;

culty.; as by afking, feeking, knocking, and that, in fome
at leaft, before they are born again, there is a kind of repentance going before, together with a forrow for fin, and
a change of life for the better, and a beginning of faith,
and an initial love of God, and a defire of grace. And
tho' they did not look on thefe endeavours to be of fuch
importance, as that it could be faid, we were thereby
rendered worthy of the grace of the Holy Spirit ; as
Pelagius and *Julian* profeffed : Yet they imagined, they
were an *occafion* by which God was moved, to beftow
his grace." And likewife the *remonftrants*, who write,
that " *fome work of man goes before his vivification ; namely
to acknowledge and bewail his death, to will, and defire deli-
verance from it ; to hunger, thirft and feek after life.*" He
obferves " there is little accuracy in the reafonings of
thefe men. For, 1ft. Since our nature is become like an
evil tree, it can produce no fruit truly good and acceptable to God, and do nothing, by which it can prepare
itfelf for the grace of regeneration. 2dly. It has
been found, that they, who, in appearance were, in the
beft manner difpofed for regeneration, were yet at the
greateft diftance from it, as the inftance of that young
man, Mark 19. 21, 22, very plainly fhews. 3dly. And
on the other hand, they, who had not even the leaft appearance of any preparation, as the publicans and harlots, went into the kingdom of God, before thofe who
were civilly righteous and externally religious. 4thly.
God teftifies, that in the firft approach of his grace, *he
is found of them, that fought him not, and afked not for him.*
Ifa. 65. 1. Fulgentius fays extremely well : *We have
not certainly received grace, becaufe we are willing, but grace
is given us, while we are ftill unwilling.*"

He then obferves, p. 483, upon the preparations
which have been admitted by fome of the reformed as
Perkins, Ames, and the Britifh Divines at the Synod of
Dort, " who have affigned in perfons to be regenerated,
1ft. A breaking off the natural obftinacy, and a flexibi-
lity

lity of the will. 2. A ferious confideration of the law.
3. A confideration of their own fins and offences againft
God. 4. A legal fear of punifhment, and a dread of
hell, and confequently a defpairing of their falvation,
with refpect to any thing in themfelves." Thefe, he
acknowledges, differ from the favourers of *Pelagianifm*
in the following manner, 1ft. That they are not for having thefe things to proceed from nature, but profefs
them to be the effects of the fpirit of bondage, prepar-
ing a way to himfelf, for their actual regeneration. 2dly.
That they are not for God's beftowing the grace of regeneration from a regard to, and moved by occafion of,
thefe preparations, much lefs by any merit in them;
but they imagine that God, in this manner, levels a way
for himfelf, fills up vallies, depreffes mountains and hills,
in order the better to fmooth the way for his entrance
into that foul." Upon which he obferves, "We really
think they argue more accurately, who make thefe and
the like things in the elect, to be preparations to the
further and more perfect operations of a more noble and
plentiful fpirit, and fo not preparations for regeneration,
but the fruits and effects of the firft regeneration : For
as thefe things fuppofe fome life of the foul, which fpiritually attends to fpiritual things, and are operations of
the fpirit of God; when going about to fanctify the
elect; we cannot but refer them to the fpirit of grace
and regeneration."

P. 485. If this matter be more clofely confidered, we
fhall find, that the orthodox differ more in words, and
in the manner of explaining, than in fenfe and reality.
For, the term, regeneration, is of ambiguous fignificati-
on; fometimes it is blended with fanctification, and by
regeneration is underftood that action of God, whereby
man, who is now become the friend of God, and endowed with fpiritual life, acts in a righteous and holy manner, from infufed habits. And then it is certain, there
are fome effects of the fpirit, by which he ufually prepares

pares them for the actings of complete faith and holi-
nels ; for, a knowledge of divine truths, a fenfe of mifery, forrow for fin, hope of pardon, &c. go before any.
one can fiducially lay hold on Chrift, and apply himfelf to the practice of true godlinefs.——But fometimes
regeneration denotes the firft tranflation of a man from
a ftate of death, to a ftate of fpiritual life ; in which fenfe
we take it.   And in that fenfe none of the orthodox, if
he will fpeak confiftently with his own principles, can.
fuppofe preparatory works to the grace of regeneration."

P. 489. " After a principle of fpiritual life is infufed
into the elect foul by regeneration, divine grace does
not always proceed therein, in the fame method and order.   It is poffible that for fome time, the fpirit of the
life of Chrift may lie, as it were dormant in fome (almoft
in the fame manner, as vegetative life in the feed of a
plant, or fenfitive life in the feed of an animal, or a poe-
tical genius in one born a poet) fo as that no vital operations can yet proceed therefrom, tho' favingly united
to Chrift, the fountain of true life by the fpirit.   This
is the cafe with refpect to elect and regenerate infants,
whofe is the kingdom of God, and who therefore are
reckoned among believers and faints, tho' unqualified
thro' age, actually to believe and practife godlinefs."

Doct. Le Blanc, a noted divine of the Reformed
Church in France in the laft century, tho' perhaps not
entirely friendly himfelf to the fentiments which *Van
Maftricht* has advanced upon the fubject of regeneration
and efficacious grace ; yet *allows* the general fentiments
of the reformed church to be fuch as are conformable to
his, as the following extracts fhew.   In the *Thefis* concerning the diftinction between fufficient and efficacious.
grace among proteftants : After giving the fentiments
of the Lutherans and Remonftrants, and obferving that
the Reformed generally renounce the diftinction, he thus
further explains their fentiments concerning divine grace.

Page 13.

Page 13. " It is the common opinion of all the Reformed who adhere to the fynod of Dort, that the grace of God, to which is to be afcribed the converfion of man and all the good works which follow thereupon, is effectual of *itfelf*; nor doth its efficacy in any meafure depend upon the co-operation or confent of the will of man ; fince it is the infallible caufe of that confent or co-operation. And this is agreeable to the decrees of the Synod of Dort. For that Synod condemn thofe, who teach *that God, in the work of regeneration, doth not put forth his almighty power, whereby he powerfully and infallibly determineth the will to faith and converfion : but that, fuppofing all the operations of grace, which God ufeth in converfion, man can fo refift God and the Spirit, when defigning and willing to regenerate him, and oft times actually doth fo refift, as utterly to hinder his regeneration ; and that therefore it remains in the power of man, whether to be regenerated or not.* They alfo condemn thofe who teach, *that grace and free will are joint caufes concurring together in the beginning of converfion, and that grace in the order of nature doth not precede the efficiency of the will : that is, that God doth not efficaciously affift the will of man to converfion, before the will of man moveth and determineth itfelf.* And how God effecteth a real converfion in the elect, the fame Synod thus explaineth. *He not only caufeth the gofpel to be externally preached unto them and powerfully illuminateth their minds by the Holy Ghoft, fo as rightly to underftand and difcern the things of the Spirit of God ; but by the efficacy of the fame Spirit, in his regenerating influences, He penetrateth the inmoft receffes of the foul ; openeth their clofed hearts ; fofteneth their hard hearts ; circumcifeth their uncircumcifed hearts ; infufeth new qualites into the will ; and of dead, maketh it alive ; of evil, maketh it good ; of unwilling, maketh it willing ; of difobedient, obedient ; and leadeth and ftrengthneth it ; fo that it is enabled, like a good tree, to bring forth fruit in good actions.* And in the next article they add, this operation of God is entirely fupernatural, alfo moft powerful and pleafant,

wonderful,

wonderful, fecret, and ineffable ; not lefs than, or inferior to, the power exerted in creation, or the refurrection of the dead ; fo that all they, in whofe hearts God
worketh in this wonderful manner, are certainly, infallibly, and effectually regenerated and converted."

Page 15. "Altho' the divines of the Reformed
Church agree in this, that grace worketh effectually, not
only upon the underftanding, but alfo upon the will of
man, and that the will is powerfully and infallibly turned and determined thereby to that which is good'; yet
there is fome difference among them, about the *manner*
in which grace affecteth the will ; fo that in confequence
thereof it fhould turn to God, and confent to that which
is good."

He then fpeaks of feveral, as *Teftard, Amyrald* and
Cameron, who fuppofe the will always to follow the laft
dictate of the underftanding ; and that the will is changed and renewed by a powerful illumination of the underftanding, agreeably to what is obferved by *Van Maftricht* concerning *Cameron* and others, § xxvi. "But (faith
he) other divines of the Reformed Church hold, that the
immediate operation of grace affecteth, not only the underftanding, by illuminating of it ; and infufing new
light into it ; but alfo the will, in which it really and
phyfically worketh that confent which it yields to the divine commands. This opinion Doct. *Ames* lays down
and explains in his *Bellarminus enervatus*, lib. iii^o *de gratiâ cap. 3. We hold,* faith he, *that together with moral
fuafion there is joined a real efficiency of God, by which a new
principle of fpiritual life is effectually wrought in the heart of
man, and he at the fame time excited to put forth the acts of
this life.* In the fame place he fully approves and acknowledges as his, the fentiment of Didacus Alvares,
which is that God by the affiftance of his grace doth
phyfically or after the manner of a phyfical caufe, effectually predetermine the will of the creature, fo that he
infallibly confenteth and co-operateth with God, calling

ling and inviting him. And afterwards using the words
of Alvares, he faith, that phyfically to pre-determine the
will is nothing elfe than truly, efficiently or really to
make the will infallibly to co-operate with God."

This fame author further obferves, p. 19. "That
there is a feeming contradiction in the fentiments of the
reformed ; who univerfally hold that man freely puts
forth the firft act of converfion, and yet that he is *merely*
paffive in the work of regeneration and converfion ; for,
how can the will of man freely put forth the act of converfion, and yet at the fame time be merely paffive
in converfion? Can the will be merely paffive, when it
is fuppofed to operate freely ?"

" The Britifh divines (he obferves) in the acts of the
fynod of Dort, folve this difficulty, by obferving that
converfion is to be taken in a two-fold fenfe ; 1ft. As
it denoteth the immediate work of God in regeneration :
2dly. As it denoteth the action of the man in turning
to God, by faving faith and repentance. In the work
of regeneration or converfion, taken in the firft fenfe,
according to them, man is merely paffive, nor is it in
the power of the will of man to hinder God thus immediately converting and regenerating : But in converfion, taken in the other fenfe, the will being influenced
by God, is active, and putteth forth thofe actions, in
which our converfion to God confifteth. But converfion, as it denoteth the immediate work of God, they
fay, is that whereby he regenerateth, and as it were createth anew, by an internal and wonderful operation the
fouls of his elect, who have been before exercifed and
prepared by various workings of his grace ; infufing into them a quickening fpirit, and endowing all the faculties of the foul with new qualities."

Much to the fame purpofe ('tis obferved) was the o-
pinion of the *Heffian* divines, at the fame fynod, which
ge gives us in the following words, " *The will of man, in*
the reception of fupernatural qualities or faculties and power,
and

and also in the reception of new inclinations, is merely passive:
So that the action of the Holy Spirit infusing that supernatural
power into the will, & turning & inclining the will effectually &
powerfully to faith & conversion, doth not depend upon the will
of man or any co-operation or consent of it. But to the acts of
faith, love, hope, &c. and all good exercises, a man is not merely
passive, but both passive and active, since, being influenced and
moved by the previous grace of God, and assisted by his subse-
quent grace, he is active in the exercises of faith, love, hope and
other virtues."

Doct. Ames, professor of divinity in the university of
Franaker, in his work entituled *Medulla Theologiæ* in the
chapter concerning effectual calling, from sect. 20, to
25, thus observes, " The reception of Christ, with respect to man, is either passive or active, Phil. 3. 12.
That I may apprehend that for which also I am apprehended
of Christ. The passive reception of Christ is that, by
which a spiritual principle of grace is begotten in the
will of man. Eph. 2. 5. *He hath quickened us.* For this
grace is the foundation of that relation, wherein we are
united to Christ. John 3. 3. *Except a man be born again,*
he cannot see the kingdom of God. The will is the most
proper and primary subject of this grace, because the
conversion of the will is the effectual principle of the
conversion of the whole man, Phil. 2. 13. *For it is God*
that worketh in you both to will and to do of his good pleasure.
An illumination of the mind is not sufficient to produce
this effect, because it doth not take away that corruption
which is seated in the will, nor doth it communicate
thereto, any new supernatural principle, whereby it can
convert itself. The will however, with respect to this
first reception, is not to be considered either as freely
active, nor as irrationally passive ; but as a subject capable of obeying the divine impression, 2 Cor. 4 6. *For*
God who commanded the light to shine out of darkness, hath
shined in our hearts," &c.

Mr.

Mr. Rutherford, a noted Scotch divine of the laſt century, in his *Exercitationes apologeticæ pro gratiâ divinâ*, gives his ſentiments relative to the will's following the laſt dictate of the underſtanding (which are agreeable to the ſentiments of Van Maſtricht) in the following words, p. 366.

" If the laſt judgment of the underſtanding neceſſarily and of itſelf determined the will, grace would become mere ſuaſion, nor would any internal grace be neceſſary to cure the will ; to remove the darkneſs of the mind and inſtruct it in what it is ignorant of would be ſufficient, *which is the grace of Pelagians.* And thus the mind of a reprobate perſon, by an acquired habit of faith, and by clear objective evidence, might be ſo taught (as appears to me poſſible in the preſent caſe) as to diſcern in a propoſed act of obedience, 1. The facility. 2. The pleaſure. 3. The utility ; and that the will ſhould not in the preſent caſe (as it might do) turn the mind to conſider, either the difficulty of it, or any other thing, wherein it might appear as diſagreeable, and that the will ſhould not turn the mind, from the contemplation of this act, to earthly conſiderations. In this caſe a perſon might believe, without his will's ever being healed, and perform a ſupernatural act ; nor would there be any need of taking away the heart of ſtone and putting within us a heart of fleſh. Nor do thoſe places of ſcripture, which are commonly objected here, prove the contrary, as Pſ. 9. 10. *And they that know thy name will put their truſt in thee.* : If this knowledge (ſay they) did not determine the will, it might be that they that know the name of God would not truſt in the LORD. And alſo John 4. 10. *If thou kneweſt the gift of God, and who it is that ſaith unto thee, give me to drink ; thou wouldſt have aſked of him, and he would have given thee living water.* Now if this knowledge would not determine the will to aſk living water of *Chriſt,* then the woman might have known the gift of God, and yet not have aſked living

M   water

water of him ; and fo the words of Chrift would not have been true, Anf. In fuch like propofitions', there is always underftood the phyfical agency of God; otherwife if it be taken exactly literal, it would follow that a fpeculative knowledge of the object would be fufficient for the act of faith, without the infufion of a new power, which no one will pretend."

Doct. *Burman,* profeffor of divinity in the univerfity of *Utrecht* thus obferves, relative to the infufficiency of illumination to renew the will, p. 227, of his *Theologiæ fynopfis,* "Sanctification *immediately* effects the will, which the very learned *Cameron* wrongly denied, afferting that the other faculties of the foul were rectified and perfected by the light of the underftanding, that the will is not immediately affected ; but always follows the laft dictate of the underftanding. Which are wrongly connected together ; fince the order and connection of thefe facul: ties, or the power and dominion which the underftanding exercifeth over the will, is not fuch, that the will implicitly followeth the fignal held up by the under- ftanding. Hence it happens that corruption doth, in fome fenfe, cleave more ftrongly to the will, or more deeply affects it, than it doth the underftanding ; hence the will cannot be excited, or move itfelf, according to the light of the underftanding alone. That the illu- mination of the underftanding is not fufficient, we have full proof daily from thofe who are reprobate. There muft be, over and above the illumination of the under- ftanding, an attention in the will : Which being fup- pofed the inclination of the will followeth the clear per- ception of the underftanding. But this attention is the gift of God, as appears in the cafe of Lydia. Acts 16. 14.

Both Rutherford and Burman are full in afferting the *priority* of regeneration to any gracious exercife, our *paf- fivity* therein, its being a *phyfical* and not a moral opera- tion, its irrefiftibility, &c.

Doct. *Braunius* profeffor of divinity at *Groningen* after confuting

confuting many false notions of divine grace held by
the Papists, Remonstrants, &c. such as that it consists
in moral suasion, in an external illumination, &c. he
observes, " That the grace of God ought to be conceived of as a new creation."—"That hereby, God dis-
pelleth the darkness of the mind, enkindleth the light of
truth, softeneth and bendeth the will; yea as it were
createth it anew, reproduceth it, and raiseth it from the
dead, and powerfully, and sweetly determineth it to
good, so that it most freely wills and embraces it."—
" Therefore the will of man is merely *passive* in the first
moment of the divine operation ; is passive in being
fashioned by God according to his good pleasure."—
" Hence the apostle well observes, that the will of man
with respect to the grace of God is as clay in the hands
of the potter, from whom it wholly receives it's form."
Doctrina Fiderum. p. 528, 529, 530.

With respect to an illumination of the understanding's
being sufficient for sanctification, he thus observes,
" They are wrong, who teach that sanctification consisteth only in the understanding; since it consisteth in
the understanding and will together. The understanding can exercise no dominion over the will, but is merely passive in the reception of objects, as they offer themselves : But the will chuseth what it judgeth to be best.
The understanding therefore ought to be enlightened,
that it may rightly receive objects and propose them to
the will. The will must be renewed, that it may chuse
the greatest good. Nor doth it follow, from the will's
following the last practical judgment, that the understanding only needs to be sanctified, and not the will ;
since this last practical judgment is the work of the will ;
for the will judgeth, not the understanding."

'Tis plain our author means by the understanding the simple faculty
of perception ; and when he excludes judgment from the understanding, he means the practical judgment, or that which respects our
practice, and not things merely speculative. In which sense perhaps
this opinion, which at first view appears singular, may be not wide
from the truth.

To

To thefe quotations I will add a few words from Mr. Brine, a late ingenious writer in England. Page 126, of his book, entituled, *A treatife upon various fubjects.*

"Regeneration preceeds and may be confidered, as the foundation and fpring of converfion and fanctification. For that is the principle from which both arife. Grace as a principle of fpiritual acts, is firft communicated, and from that proceed all acts of a holy fpiritual nature, both internal and external. Neither of the latter can be, until the firft is wrought. And when that is effected, both the latter certainly follow. In the firft we are merely paffive, in converfion and fanctification we are active."

P. 101. "Regeneration is the infufion of a new principle of fpiritual life. Naturally men are dead in trefpaffes and fins, and, therefore, in order to their acting in a holy and fpiritual manner, a living holy principle muft be communicated to them. Hence the faints are faid to be quickened, that is to fay, they are infpired with life. And this is a new life, and is a fpring of new actions. It is called a new heart, and a new fpirit, and a heart of flefh; grace is not our old nature made better, and excited unto fpiritual acts; but it is a new nature produced in our minds, by the infinite power and grace of God. For which reafon we are faid to be new creatures. Something now exifts in us, which had no being in our minds before. Nothing fhort of this comes up to the fcriptural account of this matter. No excitations, no impulfes, no aids, however forcible and great they are fuppofed to be, reach the intention of the holy Spirit, in thofe phrafes, which he ufes on this fubject. Befides our corrupt nature is not a fit fubject for heavenly excitations, nor is it poffible to bring it in fubjection to the obedience of Chrift. The carnal mind can never become fubject to the law of Chrift. A bitter fountain will as foon fend forth fweet ftreams, which all know is impoffible. Regeneration doth not confift

in

in acts, but in the production of a principle difposed unto actions holy and well pleasing unto God, by *Jefus Chrift*; and therefore this work is inftantaneous and wrought on the mind at once."

"By converfion I underftand, what may be called the *primary* actings of the regenerate principle. Before I proceed in difcourfing on which, I would premife two things. One is, the human mind, as it feems to me, is one rational principle of operation. The *fchools* have taught us, that there are three diftinct powers of the human foul, *viz.* The underftanding: The will; and the affections. They have done this for the fake of accuracy; in fpeaking of the diftinct actions of our minds. I much queftion whether this is according to truth in philofophy, and I can't but apprehend, that it hath not been ferviceably to the caufe of truth in divinity, particularly, in treating on the fubject now under confideration.

It feems to me, that our intelligent nature is one power, and not the fubject of different and diftinct powers, but capable of exerting itfelf, in various modes. In perception, willing, nilling, loving, hating, *&c.* The other thing I would premife is this: That grace is one fpiritual principle of operation in the foul, and not, properly fpeaking, various and diftinct habits feated in our mind; but able to exert itfelf after diverfe ways. As, in fpiritual perception, holy chufing and refufing, loving and delighting in fpiritual things, in a fpiritual manner, which are commonly fpoken of as acts of fo many different and diftinct habits of Grace in our minds; but I think, that they all proceed from one principle, as their common root and fpring. If this is true, thofe contefts, which have arifen and been litigated between *learned* men, concerning grace as having one power of the mind only for its fubject, and concerning the impropriety, of fuppofing, that the grace of faith is feated in two powers of the foul, *viz.* the underftanding and the will: I

fay,

say, if this is true, those contests may soon be issued, and that it is not, I am humbly of opinion, neither philosophy, nor religion will prove."

It should have been observed to the reader, that by the REFORMED, or the *reformed church*, foreign writers mean all denominations of Protestants, except the Lutherans (with respect to whom they are called reformed) and some heretical sects that have sprung up among them, as the *Socinians*, *Arminians*, &c.

This publication would have been rendered more compleat by quotations from Turretine and the doings of the famous Synod of Dort, had not the publisher been disappointed about procuring these books.

N. B. The Synod of Dort mentioned by Van Mastricht, Le Blanc, &c. consisted of delegates from the whole Reformed Church, was called by the States of Holland in the reign of King James the First, to consider the Arminian heresy, which was condemned by that Synod.

�֍✾✾✾✾✾✾✾✾✾✾✾✾✾✾✾✾✾✾✾✾✾✾✾

ERRATA.

Page 28. line 19. for *these* read *those*. P. 44. l. 19. after *confirms*, add *than destroys*. P. 53. l. 22. for *enabled* read *enobled*. P. 56. l. 6. for *pure* read *purer*. Ibid last line, for *their* read *the*. Before law read *the*. P. 81. l. 12. for *regeneration* read *generation*.

✾✾✾✾✾✾✾✾✾✾✾✾✾✾✾✾✾✾✾✾✾✾✾✾